This book is dedicated to my dear friends at Chick-fil-A,

who have created a culture of service and leadership

throughout their organization for over forty years.

Thanks for showing us it can be done.

It is also dedicated to my friend, Andy Stanley,

who has successfully shaped the culture at

North Point Community Church.

Finally, I dedicate it to my long-time mentor, John C.

Maxwell, who modeled how to nurture a leadership culture

long before I understood what it was. I was fortunate

enough to live in that culture and catch the "virus"

as a young leader. John—I am forever grateful.

Published in Atlanta, Georgia by Growing Leaders, Inc.
(www.GrowingLeaders.com)

ISBN: 978-0-9792940-0-6
Printed in the United States of America
Library of Congress Cataloguing-in-Publication Data

TABLE OF CONTENTS

A WORD ABOUT IMAGES

We live in a culture rich with images. You grew up with photos, TV, movies, video, Facebook, MTV, Instagram and DVDs. We can't escape the power of a visual image… and most of us don't want to.

I've learned over my career that most of us are visual learners. We like to see a picture, not just hear a word. Author Leonard Sweet says that images are the language of the 21st century, not words. Some of the best communicators in history taught using the power of the metaphor and image—from Jesus Christ and His parables to Martin Luther King Jr. and his "I Have a Dream" speech during the Civil Rights movement. "The best leaders," writes Tom Peters, "…almost without exception and at every level, are master users of stories and symbols."

Why? Because pictures stick. We remember pictures long after words have left us. When we hear a speech, we often remember the stories from that speech, more than the lines used by the speaker, because they painted a picture inside of us. They communicate far more than mere words. In fact, words are helpful only as they conjure up a picture in our minds. Most of us think in pictures. If I say the word "elephant" to you, you don't picture the letters: e-l-e-p-h-a-n-t. You picture a big gray animal. Pictures are what we file away in our minds. They enable us to store huge volumes of information. There's an old phrase that has stood the test of time: A picture is worth a thousand words. It was while pursuing a college degree in commercial art that I recognized the power of images. Now I get to combine my love of leadership with the power of pictures. I trust they'll impact you profoundly as they have me.

Each image in this book represents a principle you can carry with you the rest of your life. They are truths I wish someone had told me before I entered my career. Most are simple, but each is profound if put into practice. They're all about the soft skills you need to succeed at work. In nationwide surveys, employers continue to reiterate that they're desperately looking for new professionals who possess "soft skills." Hard skills are important—abilities like computing, analyzing and strategic planning—but soft skills differentiate employees who have them: work ethic, great attitudes, teamwork, empathy and communication. For some, the step from a campus to a career feels like a cross-cultural experience. In the same way you feel a little out of place when you travel to a different country, the move from backpack to briefcase may seem like a journey to a foreign land with new values, people, language and customs. The book is designed to be a map to guide you, furnishing pictures to discuss with a community of people. It's part of a series I encourage you to go through in a group. Each picture contains layers of reality, and your discussion can go as deep as you allow it to go. It's a guide for your leadership journey.

Some sociologists describe this generation as EPIC: Experiential, Participatory, Image-rich and Connected. I agree. So each of these books provides you not only with an image, but a handful of discussion questions, a self-assessment and an exercise in which you can participate. Dive in and experience each one of them. My hope is that they become signposts that guide you, warn you, and inform you on your leadership journey.

Dr. Tim Elmore

IMAGE ONE

[The Joshua Problem]

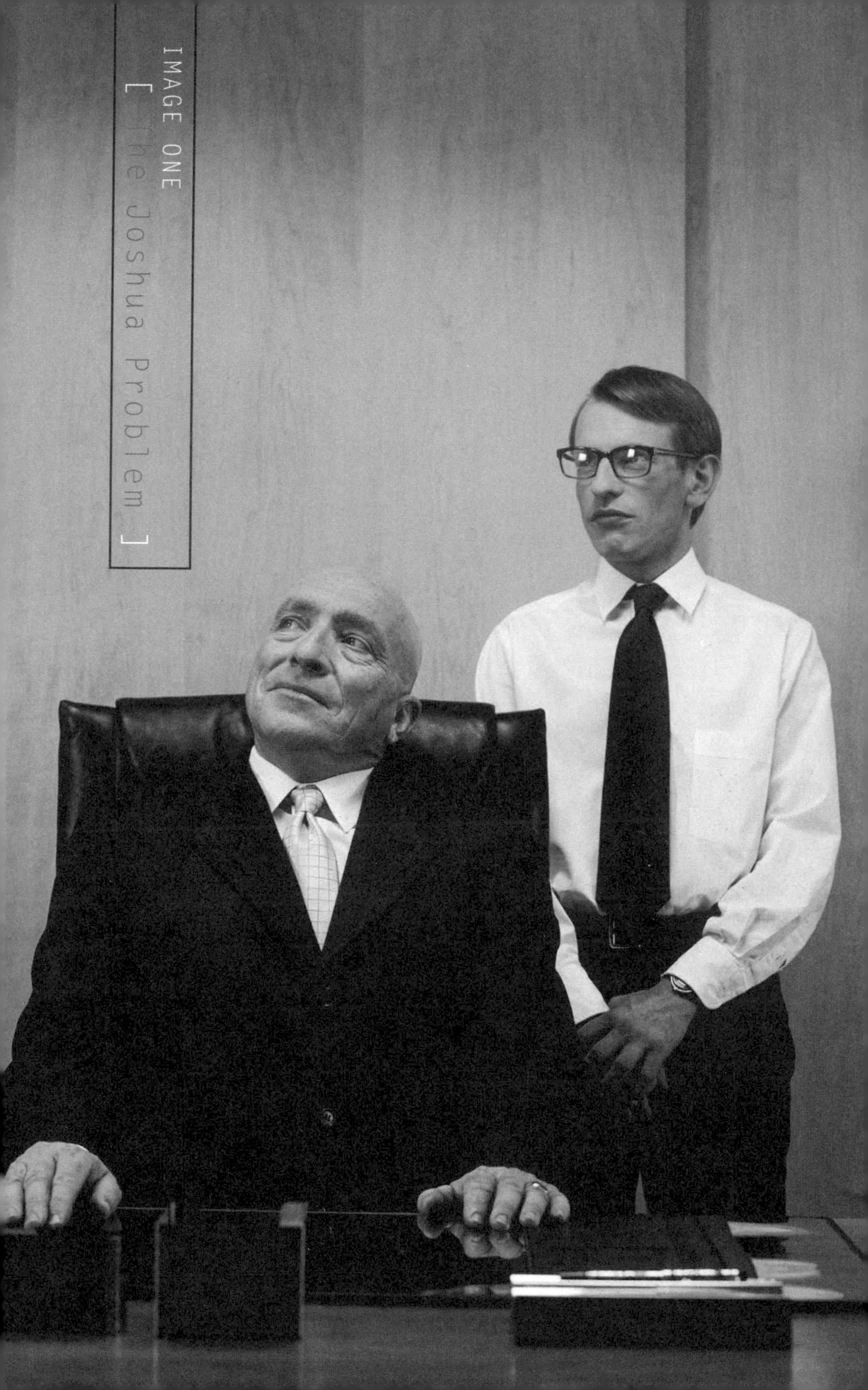

The Joshua Problem

MOSES TRAINED JOSHUA AS AN APPRENTICE. SADLY, JOSHUA NEVER TRAINED A
JOSHUA. LEADERS MUST SEE THAT A CENTRAL PART OF THEIR JOB IS TRAINING
THE NEXT GENERATION TO LEAD BEHIND THEM. LEADERS MULTIPLY.

Four thousand years ago, the greatest Jewish leader in the world was a man named
Moses. If you've never read about him—my guess is you've seen the movie. Cecil
B. DeMille directed the classic film decades ago called *The Ten Commandments*,
in which Charlton Heston played the lead role of Moses, the Patriarch of Israel.
It was unforgettable.

In the story, Moses leads the people of Israel out of slavery in Egypt, through
the wilderness, right up to the banks of the Jordan River. At this point, he stops.
He doesn't finish the job of taking the Hebrew population into the "Promised
Land." He is old and gray and ready to die. Fortunately, for several years Moses
had equipped an apprentice named Joshua. Once Moses passed away, Joshua
took the reins of leadership and led the people across the river into the land
flowing with "milk and honey." He was ready for the job and consequently, the
nation of Israel didn't have to slow down one step as they crossed the Jordan
and claimed the land God had promised them. Although it took years, one
by one, they entered the cities and began to settle. Thank God Moses had a
"Joshua" to finish the job he was unable to complete.

The problem was—Joshua didn't have a Joshua. As far as we can tell from the
reading of Scripture and other contemporary writings, Joshua never duplicated
the gift Moses had given him. He never took a young leader under his wing and
prepared him to lead. Sadly, when Joshua died, Israel entered the worst period
of her history—the period of the Judges—where twice we read:

> *"And there was no king in Israel in those days and everyone did what was
> right in his own eyes."*

> *Judges 17:6; 21:25*

Why is it we see this dilemma—this Joshua Problem—repeated thousands of times each year in organizations around the world? I don't know if leaders are just lazy, or ignorant or shortsighted, but many of them last one generation, then leave their teams in shambles, wishing their leader was still around. As we ponder changing the culture we live in, our first consideration must be the development of next-generation leaders. Leaders are carriers of the culture. I believe we must be biased toward leader development. Unless we are, we'll take the easy route and focus on our tasks at hand. The "urgent" will replace the "ultimate." Dwight Moody once said, "It's better to train a hundred men than to do the work of a hundred men. But it is harder."

LEADERSHIP CULT OR CULTURE?

In our turbulent world today, organizations tend to focus on finding and hiring one great leader to take them to the next level. Everyone seems to be looking for a "Moses" to lead them to their Promised Land. Far too often, if they find that special leader he or she becomes irreplaceable. Unfortunately, when a leader is hired from the outside rather than being developed from within the company, the organization inevitably will face another talent crisis when the leader departs. "Twenty years ago," says Jeff Sonnenfeld, associate dean at Yale School of Organization and Management, "only 7 percent of U.S. firms hired CEOs from the outside. Now it's 50 percent." We tend to just plug holes rather than meet the real need of building leaders. It's time we get out of crisis management and prevent this problem. We must build a fence at the top of the cliff rather than a hospital at the bottom.

When key leaders fail to develop other leaders, and maintain control themselves—the organization tends to look more like a *leadership cult* than a *leadership culture*. Everyone looks to the leader for answers: for vision, for encouragement, and for resources. It's all about the leader. They become a "Moses" for the team. What folks fail to realize is that Moses' greatest achievement might have been the years he invested mentoring young Joshua. Somehow he knew what Dr. Carl Henry has summarized so well: "Success without a successor is a failure."

A LEADERSHIP CULTURE:
> *At "Growing Leaders" we define a leadership culture as an environment of shared values, behaviors and language that contagiously affects team members to think and act like authentic leaders.*

A study by Stanford researchers Jim Collins and Jerry Porras found that organizations that maintained stellar performance and endured through the 20th century had one essential ingredient: a culture of succession management. In short, they developed a leadership culture rather than a personal cult of one leader.

Collins and Porras went on to write their best-selling book, *Built To Last*, reporting that visionary companies like Procter and Gamble, General Electric, Wal-Mart, 3M, and Sony preserve their culture by developing, promoting, and carefully selecting home-grown talent. The organization is a training ground for leaders, not just a retailer that sells merchandise. They don't just do programs or distribute products—they develop people.[1]

Tesco, one of the world's most admired grocery store chains, achieved leadership in the U.K. market under CEO Ian McLaurin. When he retired, some predicted that Tesco would go into decline. Instead, under the leadership of Terry Leahy, it has gone from strength to strength. They are now successful in Eastern Europe and Asia.[2] Why? Terry and others like him had been groomed at Tesco, so they would be ready at any moment to lead. Leaders are at every level.[2]

In 2005, the Disney empire said goodbye to Michael Eisner. Many thought they would have to look outside for a new leader who could handle such an amazing company. Despite great candidates like Meg Whitman from eBay, Terry Semel from Yahoo, and Paul Pressler from the Gap, Disney's board realized they had great leaders right under their nose. Disney concluded that leaders and organizations (just like all species) reproduce after their own kind. So, they hired Disney veteran Robert Iger. He breathed the culture at Disney, after being groomed for nine years.[3] It worked like a farm club for Major League baseball players. Each management experience was designed to prepare team members for the next level—from Single A, to Double A, to Triple A, to the Majors. Bob Iger was ready. He was simply a "Joshua" ready to take the lead at Disney.

BUILDING THE FARM CLUB

So what does a "Moses" do to prepare a "Joshua"? This entire *Habitudes* book is about changing a culture, and to do that, you'll have to multiply leaders who will be the carriers of the culture. However, for now I want to focus on some practical "gifts" a leader can give to a potential leader in the organization. In addition to forming work teams, try meeting in groups of four to ten people for leadership mentoring. In these clusters, give away these gifts:

1. **ACCOUNTABILITY** – Gain permission to talk about their growth and help them stay committed.

2. **ASSESSMENT** – Evaluate their present state, providing perspective on strengths and weaknesses.

3. **ACCEPTANCE** – Empower them to be themselves and not try to imitate the strengths of others.

4. **ADVICE** – Furnish words of direction, wise counsel and options as they make decisions.

5. **Affirmation** – Offer encouragement and support for them as they stretch in new areas.

6. **Admonishment** – Lend words of caution, warning them about pitfalls and correcting mistakes.

7. **Assets** – Provide tangible resources you have such as books, CDs, articles, personal contacts.

8. **Application** – Give them first-hand experiences and opportunities to apply what they learn.

Years ago, the late Dr. Nathaniel Bowditch became a ship captain by the age of twenty. That's quite a feat in itself. Fortunately, Nathaniel didn't consider this his crowning achievement. He was determined to fill the oceans with competent sailors. At twenty-one years old, he sailed on an East Indian voyage. It was on that trip he took the pains to instruct every crew-member on board in the art of navigation; he mentored them in how to lead a ship. Afterward, every sailor on that voyage became a captain of his own ship. What's more, many of those captains went on to train others.[4] There was no "Joshua Problem" here. He built his career on this belief: "I start with the premise that the chief goal of the leader is not to build followers, but to build more leaders."

A Look at the Book

Check out Numbers 27:18-23. In this passage, Moses turns over his leadership of Israel to Joshua. Notice how God instructs him to do it. Moses is to provide Joshua with his:

1. **Endorsement and authority (v.18-20)**
   Moses laid his hands on him as the people watched.

2. **Experience and opportunities (v.21)**
   Moses let him make decisions and lead the priests.

3. **Equipping and instruction (v.22-23)**
   Moses passed on the instruction God had given him.

Question: How do you think this preparation helped Joshua get over his anxiety?

_____

_____

_____

QUESTION: In what other ways did Moses help Joshua prepare as a young leader? (Exodus 17:9-14; Exodus 33:7-11; Numbers 11:28) Also, notice how Moses prepared other leaders in Exodus 18.

_____

_____

_____

QUESTION: Why do you think Joshua failed to repeat this mentoring relationship in others?

_____

_____

_____

GETTING PERSONAL

Think of the last potential leader you mentored. Evaluate how you did with these four practices:

CONVERSE
Did you discuss any principles you wanted them to learn?

< NEVER   1   2   3   4   5   6   7   8   9   10   OFTEN >

SHADOW
Did you allow them to follow you around and watch you practice leadership?

< NEVER   1   2   3   4   5   6   7   8   9   10   OFTEN >

APPRENTICE
Did you allow them to take on responsibilities as an apprentice under your care?

< NEVER   1   2   3   4   5   6   7   8   9   10   OFTEN >

DEBRIEF
Did you take time to follow up and evaluate their progress?

< NEVER   1   2   3   4   5   6   7   8   9   10   OFTEN >

PRACTICING THE TRUTH

Pray this week, and choose one potential "Joshua" that you could invest in. Invite them to meet with you on a regular basis and experience the four practices above. Talk about how well you do these four practices. Discover what other "gifts" they need in order to become a confident leader.

Critical Mass

INSIDE THE ATOMIC BOMB YOU WILL FIND U235 AND UNSTABLE TNT. WHEN
IGNITED, IT IMPLODES BEFORE IT EXPLODES. BEFORE A GROUP EXPLODES, A
LEADER MUST IMPLODE INTERNALLY WITH A FEW IN THE GROUP. START SMALL.
FOCUS ON KEY PEOPLE.

Critical mass is a term people use quite often in the corporate world today. What most individuals don't realize is that it didn't start as a business term at all. It is a term that emerged with the atomic age. When the first nuclear bomb was constructed and tested, an interesting fact came to light. The team of nuclear physicists began explaining to the public how the bomb worked. They reported that Uranium 235 was inside the shell. When mixed with TNT, it became unstable and imploded within the shell before it exploded outside the shell in that huge mushroom cloud we've all seen in photos. It's quite impressive.

What the nuclear physicists didn't recognize was they were providing a vivid analogy for how ideas catch on among groups of people. When a leader wants to transform a large organization—they often make the mistake of thinking they can stand up in front the entire bunch of them, announce the change, and hope that everyone will buy in... just because they declared it. Hmmm. It's been my experience that lasting change usually doesn't work this way. It's rare for leaders to broadcast changes and get buy-in instantly. Instead, smart leaders use the idea of "critical mass." They realize it will take time to make lasting changes, so they select a small group of key, influential people and over several weeks or months, they interact with the group about the new idea. They allow those influential people to weigh in on the idea, and take ownership of it. Those leaders understand that people support what they help create.

Finally, those key influential people go out, and either systematically or randomly create a buzz. They talk about it in their spheres of influence, with their own teams. Perhaps, they begin their own small groups to allow their people to weigh in and interact. Over time, the idea is caught. But it didn't happen overnight. It was due to the wise use of critical mass. Implosion before explosion.

Think about movements in history. In most cases, the idea of critical mass was implemented. John Wesley revolutionized England in the 1700s by using critical mass. He rode his horse around Great Britain preaching to the masses about spiritual transformation. Some of the people began responding to his message. He wisely placed them in small groups called "class meetings." They met on a regular basis, discussing the ideas and truths that Wesley had proclaimed to them. They held each other accountable to practice them. Over time, England was changed. In fact, one history book reported that Wesley almost single-handedly saved England from a bloody revolution (the kind that France and America endured during that same period) through his work. He changed the way people lived; how they worked; how they felt about slavery and how they voted. In some cities, four out of five "pubs" closed down after he preached there.

Now here's the surprising part about the transformation. Historians tell us that only 1½ to 2 percent of the British population was even on board with Wesley's "Methodist" movement. Do you realize how encouraging this statistic is? One man instigated big change through a small group who whole-heartedly bought into an idea.

During the 1800s, the abolitionist movement in America began with a relatively small group of people. Keep in mind, slavery was commonly practiced among developed nations. It was normal for English, French and Americans—even good Americans—to own slaves. But a handful of people began to re-think the ideas of American freedom. They had heard about William Wilberforce in England who had stirred up the abolition movement in the U.K. They decided they would meet as a group and debate the issue. Eventually, they got other groups to meet. Finally, it became a movement that culminated in the Civil War—and the Emancipation Proclamation by President Abraham Lincoln in 1863.

During the 1900s, Dr. Martin Luther King, Jr. spearheaded the Civil Rights movement. During a ten-year period between 1955 and 1965, African-Americans, Hispanics and Whites marched and demonstrated peacefully in the U.S. Most of it happened in the Southeast. In 1963, Dr. King made a speech on the steps of the Lincoln Memorial; it was the most famous speech of that century: "I Have a Dream." It was televised nationwide. Many citizens for the first time really understood what those folks were about. Within one year, new Civil Rights legislation was passed in America. Once again, the astounding truth about this movement is—only one percent of the U.S. population was actually on board with the movement. But that's all it took. A small group can make a big difference if that group is fully committed. This is the paradox of an epidemic: in order to create one contagious movement, you often have to create many small movements first. Implosion before explosion.

Who Do You Look For?

The logical question at this point is: who are the key people you must enlist in order to make the implosion become an explosion? Critical mass represents a percentage of the whole, and it should include key people of influence. But is there something more? In his fascinating book, *The Tipping Point*, Malcolm Gladwell thinks so. He suggests three types of people to implode with that will generate an explosion:

Mavens
Mavens are data banks. They are people who know a bit about everything. Others seek them out because they store so much information inside of them. They provide the message.

Connectors
Connectors are social glue. They spread the message because they keep such a large network of relationships. They are connected to all kinds of people who each have their own circles.

Sales People
Sales people are persuaders. They don't know as much information as mavens, but what they do know, they sell well. They're convincing, and move others to a decision.[1]

When selecting your influential people, it is optimal to include some from each of these types. Obviously, some ideas, trends or movements can happen unintentionally. But they almost always have these same types of influential people. For example, Hush Puppy shoes have been around for decades. They were a dying brand of suede shoes by the 1980s. In fact, Owen Baxter and Geoffrey Lewis had decided to phase out the antiquated shoe due to lack of sales. But in 1994, Baxter and Lewis ran into a stylist from New York who told them the classic shoe had suddenly become hip in the clubs and bars of downtown Manhattan. It made no sense to anyone. By the fall of 1995, designers and key retailers were asking to feature the shoe in their spring collection. Sales went from 30,000 pairs of shoes a year to 430,000 pairs—all within 26 months.

So how did it happen? It was estimated that the original group of people who started the fad was somewhere between 10 and 25 people. But they were the right people—fashion influencers in N.Y. They caused a $30 pair of shoes to go from a handful of Manhattan hipsters and designers to every mall in America within two years.[2] That's an amazing jump. Hmmm. What might happen if we could corral this idea and become deliberate about it, like John Wesley or Martin Luther King, Jr.? The keys are simple: Start small. Select people. Stay focused. Be patient. Remain committed. Anthropologist Margaret Mead once wrote: "Never doubt that a small group of people can change the world. Indeed, it's the only thing that ever has."

A Look at the Book

Check out Mark 3:13-19. The passage tells us that Jesus deliberately chose twelve men to become His team. What a small group of guys to impact the world within two generations. From a divine perspective, this was a God thing. In other Gospel accounts, we learn He prayed all night and selected the men His Father directed Him to choose. From a human perspective, I wonder if within that eclectic team of twelve guys, there were mavens, connectors and sales people.

1. See Acts 2:14-41. This is one instance where the few became the many. How did it happen?

_____

_____

_____

2. See Acts 3:1-4:4. Here's another instance when the number of believers grew. What happened?

_____

_____

_____

3. Check out 2 Timothy 2:2. What do we learn about selecting people to influence others?

_____

_____

_____

Getting Personal

Evaluate yourself. When you want a big change to take place among a large group of people, are you prone to try to change them all at once, or work within a small group of key people? Assess yourself on the scale below:

I WANT IT NOW   I AM WILLING TO BE PATIENT

<   1   2   3   4   5   6   7   8   9   10   >

I WORK WITH THE ENTIRE GROUP   I WORK WITH A SMALL GROUP

<   1   2   3   4   5   6   7   8   9   10   >

PRACTICING THE TRUTH

Imagine you're in charge of leading a major change in your organization. Take a pad of paper and list the key mavens, connectors and sales people you'd want to be part of your critical mass. Then, with your pad of paper, plan the "process" you would experience with this small team of people in order to implode before you explode on the entire organization. What steps would you take? How much time would you invest? How would you utilize the small core to impact the entire group?

HOLLYWOOD

PRODUCTION

DIRECTOR

CAMERA   SCENE   TAKE

HOLLYWOOD

PRODUCTION

DIRECTOR

CAMERA   SCENE   TAKE

The Hollywood Effect

WHEN LEADING CHANGE, IT TAKES YEARS TO TRANSFORM AN ORGANIZATION BY
SIMPLY CHANGING THE VALUES. IT TAKES JUST THREE YEARS BY MOBILIZING THE
LEADERS TO ACT OUT THE VALUES UNTIL THEY BECOME REALITY.

In 2006, the movie *Miami Vice* was released around the world. It's the story of two
rugged cops who use unconventional methods to get their job done. The movie
was actually a re-make of a 1980s television show, which starred Don Johnson as
Sonny Crockett. Don Johnson was "the man" back in his day. He was cool. He was
tough. He shot straight, which may explain his behavior one day, off camera. Don
Johnson had just returned to his hotel, after shopping a bit. He was enjoying some
down time, away from his hard work as an actor. As he entered the room, he saw a
thief rifling through his fiancés purse. The man had just robbed the place and was
determined to get away with his loot. Sadly for him, he had no clue whose room
he was in. When Don Johnson saw the thief he didn't have to think twice. His
well-rehearsed Sonny Crockett role clicked right in. He took off after the crook,
wrestled him to the ground and held the thief until police came to arrest him. One
bystander commented, "It was an amazing situation, just like the show!"[1]

You can only imagine what the thief felt when he looked up at his captor—only
to see the face of Mr. Miami Vice, himself. When newspapers reported the story
the next day, one consistent question surfaced over and over: "Does life imitate
TV or does TV imitate life?"

The fact is, both are true. Don Johnson had so embraced the character he played
over and over, it was intuitive for him to pursue the criminal that day. It was second
nature. He probably did it without thinking. He had "acted" his way into a character,
full-time.

This little incident illustrates an important truth for us as leaders. It's the power
of acting, from the inside out. A Russian theater director named Konstantin
Stanislavski captured the idea more than a hundred years ago. Konstantin came
up with a system for training actors, which included two major ideas: "Active
Memory" and "The Method of Physical Action."

The first theory helped actors to step into a character by utilizing their memories of past similar emotions. They were required to think of a moment in their own lives when they had felt a desired emotion and then replay that emotion in their role to achieve a more genuine performance. In other words, become the character from the inside out.

The second theory, called The Method of Physical Action (MPA), is simple to explain but its implications are profound. It is based on the idea that our emotional life is a two-way street. The only thing an actor has complete control of is his body; nothing more. Therefore, an actor must use his body as the primary tool of creation. Acting on an emotion gives it life. Actors must figure out what an emotion would cause them to do if they experienced it—and do it. The action brings out the heart and soul of that emotion.[2] To put it in common language, you are more likely to act your way into a feeling than to feel your way into an action. There is power in raw action.

So, what's our point of application? When we set out to transform a culture, we must remember that all cultures act on values they embrace. Kenya or Uganda, for instance, are countries whose citizens act a certain way because they've been raised with certain cultural values from childhood. No mother in Kenya has to tell her children to "act like a Kenyan." Why? They are living in a Kenyan culture. They will pick it up by watching the actions of those around them. In the same way, all organizations act a certain way because certain values have been embraced over time, either by default or design. They can be healthy or unhealthy, based on the conduct of those who have influence. Soon, the actions permeate the entire staff.

Research Says...

Research done by Dean Meyer and Associates helps us understand this principle. Dean and his team discovered that when a company determines to change their culture, they often make a list of the new values, then verbally communicate them to their teams. This isn't bad, but their research shows that by approaching change this way, it will take between 10 and 15 years for the organization to actually embrace those values. However, if the top leaders create a set of new values, then attach actions to each of those values and incorporate them into the leadership behavior, it requires just three years to bring about a culture change. Once again, it's the power of action. I call it The Hollywood Effect. Although it feels like you're "pretending" in the beginning, action translates faster than great speeches. Action produces emotion. And emotions multiply. They change organizations from the inside out.

Psychologist George W. Crane became known for a case he handled with a female client. The woman came to see Dr. Crane and told him she hated her husband and wanted to divorce him. She told the psychologist how selfish her husband was, and said she wanted to hurt him as badly as possible.

"Well, in that case," replied Dr. Crane, "I'd advise you to start showering him with compliments. Make him his favorite meals and serve him in any way you can. Do all you can to communicate you love him, and when you've become indispensable to him, then present the divorce papers to him. This is the best way to hurt him deeply."

Dr. Crane sent her off and asked her to call in a few months to let him know when she was ready to begin the divorce proceedings. Interestingly, she never called. When Dr. Crane finally spoke to her and asked if she was ready for the divorce—she emphatically resisted. "Divorce him?" she responded. "I changed my mind. When I began acting like I loved him, I discovered I really did."

Aristotle wrote, "Men acquire a certain quality by constantly acting a certain way. You become just by performing just actions. You become temperate by performing temperate actions, brave by performing brave actions."

Surely there's a principle here for leaders who want to transform their organizational culture. We can't just talk about it, or hold conferences, or even post some new set of values on the wall. We must act the way we want our culture to be—even if it feels like we're pretending at first. We must become the change we desire. We can't afford to wait until we "feel" like it. Remember, we're more likely to act our way into a feeling than to feel our way into an action. Along the way, it'll become second nature, just like Don Johnson stopping a thief on the street. It's The Hollywood Effect.

A Look at the Book

1. Jesus celebrated this truth more than once. He affirmed those who acted in faith on what He said. Check out Luke 6:46. In this passage, Jesus assumes something about His followers. What is it?

_____

_____

2. In the next three verses, 47-49, Jesus tells a story about two builders. What's the difference between the two of them?

_____

_____

_____

3. In Matthew 21:28-31, we read the story of a father and two sons. Both sons were asked to do something, but each had different responses. What was the big difference? Which did Jesus affirm? Why?

_____

_____

_____

4. In 1 Samuel 17, we read the classic story of David and Goliath. It is an illustration of The Hollywood Effect. David's action affected the whole Israeli army. Contrast the army before David acted and after.

_____

_____

_____

5. In Joshua 24:14-18 we see another example of The Hollywood Effect. How did Joshua's example affect the people of Israel?

_____

_____

_____

GETTING PERSONAL

Take a moment and list your organization's top six values below:

1. _____   4. _____

2. _____   5. _____

3. _____   6. _____

Now—honestly evaluate how well you model those values for your team. Do you act on them?

_____

_____

_____

Practicing the Truth

Choose one of the values in your list above that you feel you don't model well. Make it a project to begin acting on that value, to see how it affects the people around you. Try the following steps:

1. Identify a person who does model the value well and interview them. Learn from them.

2. Brainstorm specific ways you can practice the value at work, school or at home.

3. Pray about this value, asking God to enable you to incarnate it into your life.

4. Read a book about that particular value.

After a week, evaluate whether anyone noticed a change in you. Did your actions positively affect anyone?

_____

_____

_____

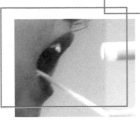

Family Virus

CULTURES WORK LIKE A VIRUS IN A FAMILY. VIRUSES ARE CONTAGIOUS BECAUSE
FAMILY MEMBERS ARE SIMILAR AND LIVE CLOSE TOGETHER. LEADERS HIRE THE
CULTURE THEY WANT AND FOSTER CLOSE RELATIONSHIPS AND TEAMWORK.

A horrifying news report was broadcast in May, 2006. It all took place in Jakarta, Indonesia. The mother of a large family was unknowingly exposed to a bird flu virus as she sold vegetables at the market. The virus was carried by chickens in the station next to hers. When she returned home at the end of the day, the woman greeted each of her family members. Everything seemed quite normal. By the next morning, however, each of her family members began to suffer from symptoms of the bird flu. Within weeks, six of seven family members were dead.

Doctors and scientists who studied this bird flu epidemic noticed something quite intriguing. None of the other family members were exposed to the chickens in the marketplace, so experts concluded that the virus spread through this woman. Although the deaths in that family cluster were the largest ever reported, the outbreak could have been larger. Fortunately, the virus did not spread outside the family, even though the woman was in contact with other people. In other words, not everyone she touched caught the virus. So there had to be another factor than just proximity that caused the deaths. Scientists soon concluded what that factor was. In all the family clusters that were infected, only direct blood relatives—not spouses—caught the bird flu. This means the virus was contagious for two major reasons: proximity and similar genetics.[1]

This story can be told a hundred times over across the globe. Viruses are caught due to the same two reasons—people are *close* and they are *comparable*. Proximity and similarity. This illustrates another *Habitude* which teaches us how leaders spark movements and epidemics. I call it "family virus." A culture is nurtured quickly when people work closely to each other, and they share a common make up. In fact, we can take it a step further. All cultures give birth to people already like the culture, and the people within a culture become more like each other by working together in teams.

A virus can be contagious and infectious, and it can actually cause an epidemic if placed within the right context. People of the same blood who live in proximity to one another are the most susceptible. Take the act of yawning for example. Picture someone yawning as they sit among a group of people. Have you ever noticed how when one person yawns, it often prompts others nearby to begin yawning too? Yawning is a surprisingly powerful act. It is contagious. And it is especially contagious within people who share a similar make up. It's a classic example of "family virus."

On a more tragic note, sociologist David Philips, from UCSD, has studied what he calls a "suicide virus." David has studied famous suicide stories reported on the front page of newspapers, during a twenty-year stretch between the 1940s and the 1960s. Then, he matched them up with suicide statistics from the same period of time. He found that immediately after stories of suicides made the news, there was a jump in the number of suicides in those areas.[2] For some reason, suicides are infectious. And this kind of contagion isn't rational like a persuasive argument. It's the power of suggestion.

"When I'm waiting at a traffic light and the light is red, sometimes I wonder whether I should walk or jaywalk," Philips writes. "Then, somebody else does it and so I do it, too. It's a kind of imitation. I'm getting permission to act from someone else who is engaging in a deviant act." Somehow we feel better when we're not acting alone. For some reason, we trust someone else's judgment more than our own, whether it is jaywalking or driving fast on the freeway. Behavior can be viral.

So, how can we put this *Habitude* to work as leaders? Let me suggest the following ideas. First, ideas, products, messages and behaviors spread like viruses through repeated exposure. Leaders can harness this by summarizing a contagious message and exposing their team to it repeatedly.

Viruses grow exponentially, doubling over and over as they spread. Once something gets started, repetition can make it multiply until it gains momentum and becomes more attractive than it deserves to be. I'm sure you've heard of books or movies or trends that have become wildly popular, and you've thought to yourself: how could such a simple thing spread so fast? It's easy. Family virus. Leaders must consistently talk about the idea they want to spread, and keep their people close together until it catches on. A contagious idea or vision has three requirements:

1. YOU MUST SEE IT CLEARLY

2. YOU MUST SHARE IT CREATIVELY

3. YOU MUST SAY IT CONSISTENTLY

Second, viruses expand among people who share the same values. So, leaders must hire the culture they want. New employees should match the desired culture and have chemistry with their team members. Chick-fil-A restaurants are a great example of these concepts. Recently, I spoke with Tim Tassopoulos, an executive with Chick-fil-A in Atlanta. When I asked him how they've nurtured such a contagious leadership culture, he said simply: "At this point, we hire the culture." They not only groom leaders from within who've already caught the "virus," they only hire or promote people who incarnate the culture. They often invest several months in interviews before they hire a store operator. They treat the hiring process more like a "marriage" than a "date." Think about it. You might say yes quickly to someone who asks you out on a date, but you'd take a lot more time getting to know them if they proposed marriage! Consequently, their employee retention rate is over 93 percent. And the people who join the team already think and act like the "culture."

David Salyers, vice president of marketing at Chick-fil-A, once told me how he got the promotion to his position. Truett Cathy, the founder of Chick-fil-A, met with him in his office. Truett and the rest of the executive team affirmed David's potential to serve as vice president. Nevertheless, they added, there was just one change they required of him. David responded he was willing to do whatever was necessary for the promotion. He was shocked, however, at their request. They told him: "You're spending too much time at the office." He couldn't believe his ears, but he had heard them correctly. The executives felt David was spending too much time at the office and not modeling balance in his life. They reminded him how contagious leaders are and how they couldn't afford making him a leader if he passed on unhealthy work habits. Many of his staff had families and the executives didn't want a leader who infected them with the idea that they should work late into the night. Wow. It isn't often you see a company who understands how infectious a culture can be, and is willing to set standards to keep the environment healthy.

How Does a Virus Get Started?

Once you understand that a "family virus" is a product of your environment and the people who pass them on, you can capitalize on your culture and make your ideas extremely infectious. To summarize, here are some action steps to take:

1. FORM TEAMS TO KEEP YOUR PEOPLE WORKING CLOSELY TOGETHER.

2. INFECT THOSE TEAMS WITH THE BIG IDEAS YOU BELIEVE WILL SHAPE THE CULTURE.

3. DEVELOP AND PROMOTE PEOPLE WHO "CATCH" THE VIRUS AND ARE CONTAGIOUS WITH THE IDEAS.

4. RESOLVE TO ONLY HIRE PEOPLE WHO ALREADY INCARNATE THE CULTURE.

5. The essentials you want in team members are: character, competence and chemistry.

Do these things well and who knows what might happen? You might even start an epidemic.

A Look at the Book

Let's look at a couple of case studies in Scripture that illustrate the power of family virus.

1. First, check out 1 Samuel 22:1-2. David is a leader on the run, in distress, attempting to escape from Saul. Notice the kinds of team members he attracts. What do we learn from them?

_____

_____

_____

2. Later, David trains these disgruntled men to become a small but mighty army. He invests in his leaders and they even become "giant killers." How do you suppose being alike and being in proximity played a role in their development?

_____

_____

_____

3. Now consider Jesus' work with the twelve men He chose to be disciples. While they came from diverse backgrounds, they all were young, hungry for change and ready to take action. Can you think of any ways this _Habitude_ can be seen in their development as a team?

_____

_____

_____

Getting Personal

Are you on a team right now? Whether you're leading it or not, evaluate how contagious your environment is, based on the truths of "family virus."

1. Do we share similar values and desires?

   < NO   1   2   3   4   5   6   7   8   9   10   YES >

2. Do we work in closely in teams?

   < NO   1   2   3   4   5   6   7   8   9   10   YES >

3. Do we embrace an infectious idea and try to pass it on?

   < NO   1   2   3   4   5   6   7   8   9   10   YES >

4. Do we only add members who incarnate the culture?

   < NO   1   2   3   4   5   6   7   8   9   10   YES >

Practicing the Truth

Try this exercise. If you're not on a team right now, imagine you're leading a team and can choose whomever you want to join that team. What's your objective? What values should be practiced? What kind of culture do you want on that team? Write these answers down. Now, consider the three ingredients of character, competence and chemistry. Who would you add to the team and why? Discuss it with a community of friends.

Portable Truths

PEOPLE DON'T CHANGE EVEN WITH GOOD INFORMATION. WHY? THEY RETAIN
TRUTH IN TRANSFERABLE CONCEPTS OR PORTABLE PRINCIPLES. LEADERS FIND
MEMORABLE LANGUAGE TO COMMUNICATE AND REPRODUCE IDEAS.

When I was growing up in the 1960s and 1970s, the dangers of cigarette smoking had just begun to catch the attention of the public. Cigarette packages were forced to include "The Warning" from the Surgeon General about how cigarettes cause lung cancer and other diseases. The tobacco industry had begun to incur lawsuits from unhealthy customers, and eventually cigarette companies were no longer allowed to advertise on TV.

But before cigarettes went off the air, Winston cigarettes did something that positioned them ahead of their competition for years to come. They began an ad campaign that people remembered. Their new slogan was: "Winston tastes good like a cigarette should." Simple. No flashy insight. But this little phrase soon became a song that stuck in people's minds. Within months, Winston surpassed leading brands like Kent, L & M, and Parliament. In fact, just months after this little phrase hit the market, Winston raced into second place as a leading brand just behind Viceroy. They kept sharing the simple phrase on billboards and in magazine ads, and in a few years it seemed that every American knew it (even non-smokers!). Winston became the top selling cigarette in America.

This illustrates another *Habitude* I believe is critical to changing the culture of an organization. Every culture has a language. China. France. Spain. England. Germany. Language is part of what separates one culture from another, and I believe leaders understand this reality. That's why effective leaders find specific ways to make their message unique and memorable—contagious. This involves both the "what" and the "how" of the communication—the content and the delivery. Leaders insure that their message is "portable" and can be grasped and passed on easily to those who hear it. People get it and they can give it away.

What's the Big Deal?

Why is this such a big deal? After all, people are not stupid. Why can't leaders just say it? The problem is not people's I.Q. The problem is information overload. We have become a society that is overwhelmed by others clamoring for our attention. Malcolm Gladwell writes that "in just the past decade the time devoted to television commercials in a typical hour of programs has grown from six minutes to nine minutes, and continues to climb every year. Media Dynamics estimates that the average American is now exposed to 254 different commercial messages in a day."[1] Furthermore, when we watch four commercials in a row, the effectiveness of the message in any one commercial drops to almost zero. Our brains have found a way to screen out information. In fact, if we didn't screen the content, we'd be paralyzed by too many messages.

This is why leaders need to use portable truths. Once they distill their key message, they discover ways to make it easy to remember and easy to reproduce in someone else. Winston Churchill did this when he described the prison of Communism as an "iron curtain." Martin Luther King, Jr. did it when he cast his vision for a free America, and said, "I have a dream." Herbert Hoover did it in 1928 when he promised Americans "a chicken in every pot and a car in every garage." The phrase becomes portable and slowly, the culture is shaped.

Painting a Picture

In each of these cases, and hundreds of others like them, leaders have been able to paint a permanent picture in the minds of their listeners that fostered a mindset; it created a culture. Good leaders harness the power of the metaphor. They use stories, colorful adjectives, parables, or other kinds of word pictures that stick—because most people think in pictures. This is why I've chosen to teach leadership principles using "*Habitudes*." Like other leaders or communicators, I hope to help people carry these images with them like luggage—lots of items packed in, but all are portable.

So, if ideas are to be portable, how does it work? How do we make them infectious? I have found that ideas or visions spread fast when they possess four characteristics:

1. THE IDEA IS DIFFERENT.
   As technology increased, email replaced fax machines and websites replaced brochures. New ideas often require paradigm shifts in people's minds. You must differentiate your idea from others. How is it unique, creative and outstanding?

2. THE IDEA IS MEMORABLE.
   Just like Winston cigarettes, leaders use phrases to share ideas that people can't shake. You must find a way to put a picture in people's minds. How is it unforgettable and catchy?

3. THE IDEA IS RELEVANT.
No one thought computers would catch on forty years ago. The reason for their success is because they met a common need to capture and communicate information. You must meet a relevant need; the idea must solve a problem. Does your idea scratch an itch?

4. THE IDEA IS SIMPLE.
Mother Teresa is quoted all the time. Why? Most of her phrases used one syllable words. You must keep the idea easy to capture and pass on. Can a middle school student get it?

Dawson Trotman used to call "portable truths" by another name. He called them "transferable concepts"—ideas that are reduced to a principle that help people remember them and share them. Dawson was the founder of the Navigators, an organization which began working with military personnel back in the 1930s. His first "student" was a sailor named Les Spencer. Dawson became a mentor for Les, and the two began studying his transferable concepts. Once they completed their study, Dawson encouraged Les to mentor someone else. What began with two people—soon became four, then eight, then sixteen, then thirty-two, then sixty-four... and so on. It was one-to-one mentoring using transferable concepts.

The bottom line? Within a few years, the Commanding Officer on board the ship thought some sort of cult had broken out among the crew. These sailors had been trained in biblical ideas and each could pass them on to others. Their lives had changed. They weren't acting like sailors any more! They had, in fact, created a different culture on the ship. The C.O. requested that the F.B.I. come on board and investigate what was happening. What the investigators found after four months of interviews was a transformed culture that started with one man[2]... and some portable truths.

A LOOK AT THE BOOK

1. Check out Matthew 13:31-35. In this text, Matthew reminds us that Jesus didn't teach anything without using a parable. They were portable truths. What advantage do parables have to become portable in people's minds? Why was it such a good way to transform the way folks think?

2. Review Matthew 6:9-13. It contains what we call "The Lord's Prayer." It is the most famous prayer, the most often recited prayer in the world—yet the whole thing is just 51 words. What makes this such a portable prayer?

_____

_____

3. Comment on Jesus' teaching and His word choices. What makes Him such an effective leader? What enables Jesus to transform a culture with His words?

_____

_____

GETTING PERSONAL

Think about a big idea you want to communicate to others. It may be an idea you wish to transfer to your team or people outside your team. Write it below:

_____

_____

_____

Now evaluate how portable your words are based on the four ingredients we listed earlier. Use a scale of 1-10, with ten being the highest:

1. IS YOUR IDEA DIFFERENT? IT IS UNIQUE, CREATIVE AND OUTSTANDING?

<   1   2   3   4   5   6   7   8   9   10   >

2. IS YOUR IDEA MEMORABLE? IS IT CATCHY? DOES IT PAINT A PICTURE?

<   1   2   3   4   5   6   7   8   9   10   >

3. IS YOUR IDEA RELEVANT? DOES IT MEET A NEED OR SOLVE A PROBLEM?

<   1   2   3   4   5   6   7   8   9   10   >

4. IS YOUR IDEA SIMPLE? IS IT EASY TO GRASP AND PASS ON TO OTHERS?

<   1   2   3   4   5   6   7   8   9   10   >

PRACTICING THE TRUTH

Take some time with your team and tweak your "big idea" you evaluated above, especially if you feel you need to improve its portability. How can you communicate the idea in a more transferable fashion? How can you say it so people will think in a new way and share it with others? Take some time and work on the idea. Then discuss your improvements with your team. Does your idea have the potential to change the culture of your organization?

Trade-Offs

EVERY DECISION IS A TRADE-OFF. DOING ONE THING MEANS YOU CAN'T DO ANOTHER. LEADERS CAN DO ANYTHING BUT THEY CAN'T DO EVERYTHING. IN DECIDING WHAT YOU'LL DO, YOU CHOOSE WHAT NOT TO DO.

My friend Dick Wynn told me about a leadership summit he attended with the famous Peter Drucker. During his career, Mr. Drucker was considered the top management guru in America. Dick told me that day was unforgettable. After a full day of providing leadership insights, Peter told the attendees to put their pens down. He reminded them that they had about ten more minutes together before the day would be over. Then, he asked them to take out a fresh piece of paper and begin writing down all the ideas they planned to implement as a result of their time together. At that point, he set them in motion. Dick told me everyone began frantically making a list of all the things they planned to apply from their wonderful training time.

With five minutes to spare, however, Peter Drucker told everyone to stop. Then he shocked them. He instructed the attendees to turn their paper over and begin making a list of all the items they would *stop doing* to make room for the new ideas they were going to start doing. Oops. Ouch. Dick told me he looked around and no one was writing anything down at first. Why? We just don't do this in today's world. We never stop doing things—we just keep adding to our "to do" list. And our lives become crazier and crazier.

The fact is, the most effective leaders have found a way to simplify their lives and their mission, and consequently their culture. They understand that all cultures must decide what's important enough to keep and what isn't. Leaders don't allow the culture to be so cluttered with every priority that people are fuzzy as to what's most important. Cultures become distinct and effective when their top leaders choose to say "no" to many things in order to keep the main thing, the main thing. They know that leaders can do anything, but they can't do everything. When they choose the "main thing" and create a culture around it, it's possible to maintain that culture more easily.

The problem is—leaders have a hard time saying "no." I know. I am one of them. When "Growing Leaders" first started, I was involved in leadership training on a number of levels: corporate leaders, international leaders, church leaders and students. While the common thread was leadership development, I was spread too thin. I realized I couldn't do it all. "Growing Leaders" had to have a sweet spot that we intentionally pursued. We finally decided we would invest our prime time in young leaders, ages twelve to twenty-four. Certainly, we have partners who use our resources outside of that window, but we pursue only the small window of the "millennial generation."

A Hard Lesson to Learn

What we've found is that shooting for one, small target has made us bigger and increased our influence, without even trying. Saying "no" caused us grow. This is the benefit of "trade-offs." It's a risk and it's counter-intuitive, at times. Logic says to do it all, so your organization can reach more people or make more money. But a refusal to make the "trade-off" can have negative effects. For instance, PillowTex Corporation was the largest pillow manufacturer in the U.S. Everyone knew them as the "pillow experts." However, they just couldn't refuse the idea of expanding into towels, sheets and rugs. Soon, both team members and customers became confused as to who PillowTex really was and what was their expertise? Their internal culture began to fade. Sales dropped. In 2003, they shut down.[1] Why? By refusing to make a "trade-off," they lost their identity and diluted their brand.

Sadly, this is a common American story: corporations lusting after growth don't see the need for a trade-off, and consequently no one—even team members—recognize who they are. They lose the culture they've worked so hard to create. Even today, Sears is refocusing with a vengeance, trying to recover from a plan to grow at any cost. Eastman Kodak sold Sterling Winthrop (Bayer aspirin) to focus on core film operations. Quaker Oats is folding its in-house promotions, design and media services to "better focus resources on building key brands."[2] All of these stories are stories of organizations being forced to make a "trade-off" in order to resuscitate a brand or a culture.

Wikipedia defines "trade-off" saying it "usually refers to losing one quality or aspect of something in return for gaining another quality or aspect. It implies making a decision with full comprehension of both the upside and the downside of that choice." The leader believes what he or she gives up is worth the price of what he or she gains. We do this every day without thinking. Board games almost always involve trade-offs. For instance, in chess, do you trade a bishop for a position you want? In Monopoly, do you trade in some money for a hotel on Park Place? In Clue, do you risk guessing who the murderer is before you have all the facts because you sense your opponent may win it all on their next turn? Good questions. When you think about it, most of life is a bunch of trade-offs. Every purchase you make in a store is a trade-off: money for products.

What makes the decision hard is that we really want both! In fact, "trade-offs" become difficult because...

1. WE DON'T WANT TO GIVE UP ANYTHING. WE WANT IT ALL.

2. WE'RE UNCERTAIN IF GIVING SOMETHING UP WILL REALLY GET US WHAT WE WANT.

3. WE WORRY ABOUT MAKING A DESTRUCTIVE DECISION THAT WE CANNOT REVERSE.

4. WE FEEL LIKE WE DON'T HAVE ENOUGH INFORMATION TO MAKE A GOOD CHOICE OR WISE RISK.

5. WE FEAR THE FACTS WE HAVE WILL CHANGE IN THE FUTURE AND OUR TRADE-OFF WILL GO SOUTH.

MAKING A GOOD TRADE-OFF

Remember, almost every decision is a trade-off. Leaders understand these decisions must not only reflect their mission, but also their culture. They must ask: Will this decision enhance our culture or dilute it? In his best-selling book, *Good to Great*, Jim Collins suggests how to make good choices about culture, mission and revenue, by introducing the Hedge Hog Concept. He says leaders must ask three questions before making organizational decisions. I have added a fourth one on culture:

1. PASSION: What are you deeply passionate about?

2. ABILITY: What can you be the best in the world at doing?

3. REVENUE: What drives your economic engine?

4. CULTURE: What is congruent with the culture you're trying to build?

The story of the Golden Gate Bridge is a beautiful tale about a trade-off. As the bridge was being built, the chief contractor grew angry as the builders fell behind schedule. It was taking his crew far too long to complete each section of the bridge and each day the deadlines seemed more unrealistic. Despite his motivation, the chief soon recognized he couldn't move them any faster. Then, it all came to a climax when the workers requested they stop and construct a net underneath to protect them if they fell. While safety was important to everyone, the last thing the chief wanted to do was take more time away from making progress on construction. They were already behind and suspending a net would postpone them even further. A trade-off stared him in the face. His choice? The chief chose to trade deadlines for safety; he felt it was worth the delay. The results were shocking. He discovered the net actually sped up construction.

Men were less concerned about their safety and could focus on their work. Hence, they worked twice as fast. As it turned out, the bridge got done on time, and everyone was safe. The trade-off turned into a great pay off.

A Look at the Book

Check out Luke 12:16-21. Jesus tells a story about a man who failed to make a wise trade-off. Take a moment and interpret what really happened, and why he failed.

1. The central figure in the story is a rich man. What were the two choices he had with his money?

_____

_____

_____

2. What was the real issue this rich man failed to see? Were his priorities in order?

_____

_____

_____

3. Why do you believe he failed to handle the trade-off well?

_____

_____

_____

4. What enables us to choose wisely when faced with a trade-off involving two good options?

_____

_____

_____

5. Leaders get in trouble when they abandon values in decisions because they feel the end justifies the means. This causes healthy cultures to become fuzzy. Have you seen this happen? When?

_____

_____

_____

Getting Personal

Using the criteria I mentioned earlier, evaluate how you make "trade-offs" as a leader:

1. Passion: How important is sticking to your area of passion? Rank its importance below.

   < LOW VALUE 1 2 3 4 5 6 7 8 9 10 HIGH VALUE >

2. Ability: How important is focusing on your area of competency? Rank its importance below.

   < LOW VALUE 1 2 3 4 5 6 7 8 9 10 HIGH VALUE >

3. Revenue: How important is knowing good income will result? Rank its importance below.

   < LOW VALUE 1 2 3 4 5 6 7 8 9 10 HIGH VALUE >

4. Culture: How important is staying true to a healthy culture? Rank its importance below.

   < LOW VALUE 1 2 3 4 5 6 7 8 9 10 HIGH VALUE >

Practicing the Truth

Meet with your leadership team and discuss this *Habitude*. Together, make a list of the values your culture celebrates and refuses to compromise. List the "core values" that help you make trade-offs more easily. Can you name the principles that help you make tough decisions? After your discussion, list them below. How does this list correspond to your personal values? Leaders are energized when their personal values align with organizational values. Complex trade-offs are simplified. Healthy cultures are a natural result. Discuss this issue with your team.

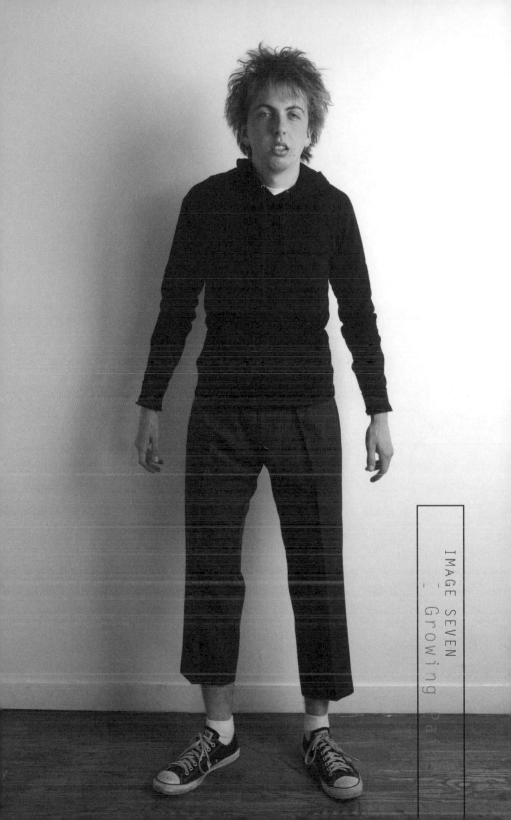

IMAGE SEVEN

[Growing Pains]

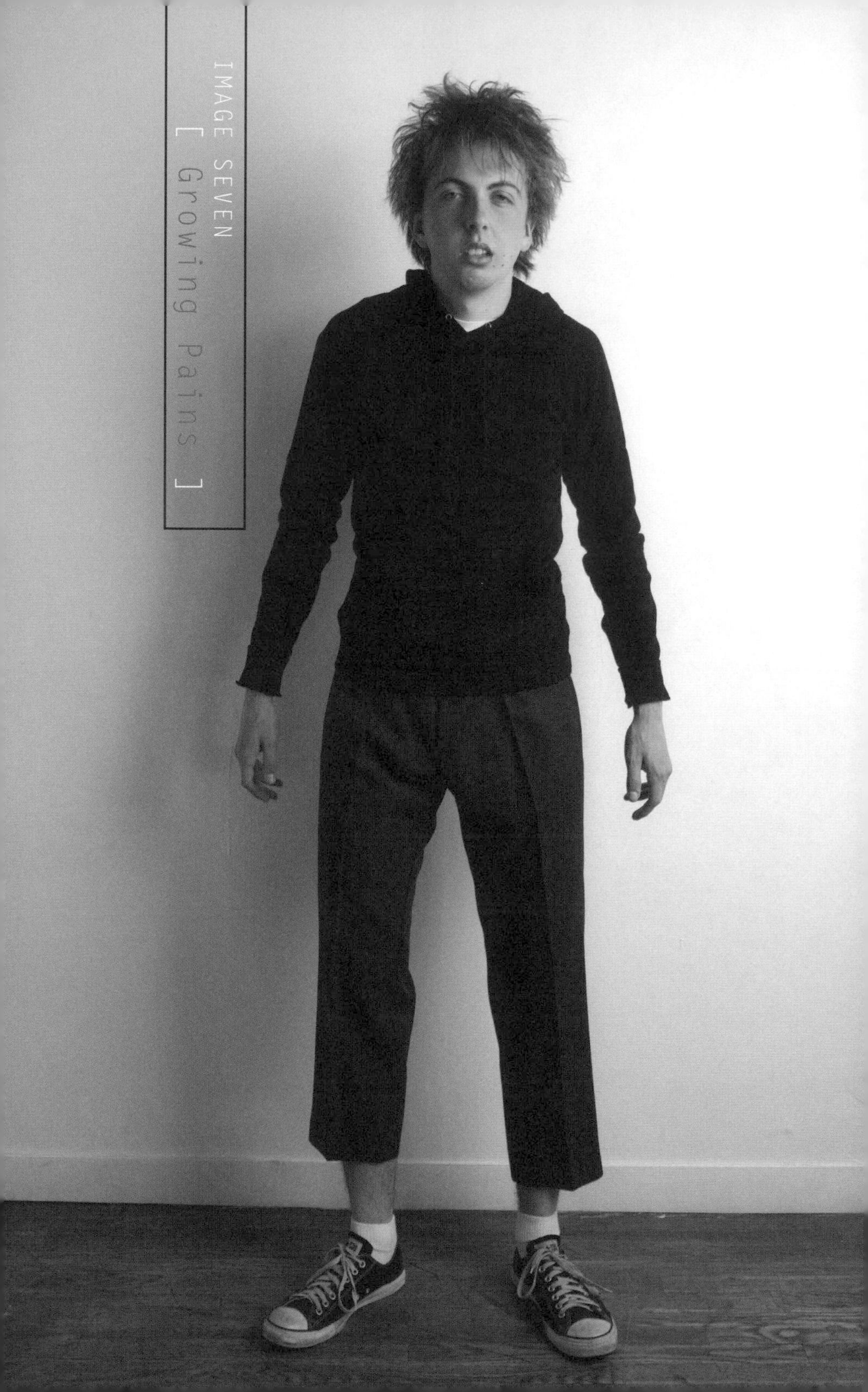

Growing Pains

PEOPLE CAN HANDLE ABOUT 20 PERCENT CHANGE A YEAR. WHEN SKILLED LEADERS LAUNCH NEW PROJECTS, THEY DON'T MAKE ALL THE CHANGES AT ONCE. IDEAS MUST BE TIMED RIGHT FOR ACCEPTANCE AND PEOPLE NEED TIME TO OWN THEM.

During my son Jonathan's thirteenth year, he physically grew several inches. In fact, my wife and I watched him grow six inches in six months. It was weird. We could literally see him grow that year. It was challenging just to keep up with his growth, buying shirts, pants and shoes that fit him. It seemed we couldn't buy Jonathan new clothes fast enough. The strangest part about his growth was the stretch marks on his legs. Yes, you read that right. Jonathan had stretch marks around his knees on both legs. He had grown so fast his skin couldn't keep up with his development. And he could feel it. Sometimes he would experience aches and pains and not know why. The only explanation my wife and I had for him was "growing pains." When he asked what in the world "growing pains" are, we simply responded, "It's the pain that results when someone grows too fast. It hurts."

There's a helpful *Habitude* in this little analogy for us. Good leadership generally results in growth for the people and institutions they lead. Healthy leaders foster healthy cultures, which cause healthy organizations. All of that leads to growth because healthy things naturally grow. Here's the catch. Wise leaders recognize that they must monitor that growth. For example, when a gardener fertilizes her garden well, she must watch what it does to the plants. A good gardener may have to prune the plant so that it doesn't grow recklessly and take over the entire garden. Unmonitored, unwatched growth can cause damage. In the same way, as we nurture the transformation of the culture around us, we must understand how it will impact the people. So—how much is too much?

THE 20 PERCENT RULE

Over time, leadership consultants have found that approximately 20 percent of your team members will lead the changes that occur within an organization. They are the pioneers and early adopters.

Additionally, the remaining members can only handle about 20 percent change per year. When a team or organization expands any faster, it normally scares people and they push back. It isn't that those people are against change—it's just that changing more than 20 percent in a year can be too much, too soon. I have watched people become emotionally paralyzed by too much change. It's as though they push a "pause button" inside and refuse to cooperate with the leadership. Like my son's stretch marks on his legs, the growth begins to hurt.

PACE NOT RACE

So, what's a leader to do? When you see your organization needs change, the temptation is to do everything at once. Wise leaders remember it's about a pace, not a race. Pace yourself by focusing on making the most important changes first, and only initiate about 20 percent of them a year. Some of the best ideas in the world weren't received well at first. Coca-Cola, for example, is the leading brand in the world. People across the globe recognize the logo as the most refreshing soft drink anywhere. But, did you know in 1886, it wasn't a refreshing soft drink at all. It was a medicine, sold in drugstores! Dr. John Pemberton created it to soothe headaches and calm nerves. The medicine was selling fairly well, when someone asked Dr. Pemberton about changing it into a drink. He wasn't too interested in the idea. Eventually, a drugstore clerk accidentally mixed some of the elixir with carbonated water instead of tap water. Soon, people noticed it was refreshing. Two years later, in 1888, folks began calling it Coca-Cola.

That's when Asa Candler suggested to Dr. Pemberton that they sell it at the soda fountain, rather than the medicine counter, to refresh shoppers. He was allowed to buy it in big red barrels and resell it to drug stores as a fountain drink, but it was limited to soda fountains in drug stores. That is, until two men approached Asa Candler with the idea of selling it in bottles. Candler thought these two guys, Mr. Thomas and Mr. Whitehead, were crazy. They persisted, and finally convinced Candler to sell them the rights to bottle it for $1.00. Suddenly, people all over America could drink Coke from a bottle at home or wherever they were. It grew popular with everyone in the U.S. In 1919, another man, Mr. Woodruff, came along with an even bigger vision for Coke. He believed it would sell all over the world. People thought he was crazy too. But he pushed his mantra: "The taste of Coke on the lips of everyone in the world."[1] He took that vision to where it is today. Almost every country has access to Coca-Cola—it's the number one drink in the world. But, it didn't happen overnight. The idea had to evolve, and it took many years to reach worldwide acceptance.

Remember, when you introduce new ideas in your organization, moving too fast may shut things down.

We've all heard of a team or organization that changed too fast. When leaders initiate too much change too quickly, people may attack you. In other words, if a captain gets too far ahead of his troops, they may mistake him for the enemy! In organizations, they may resist the discomfort or pain associated with imposed change. The symptoms of their pain can be fear, anger, frustration, resentment, distrust or anxiety. When a leader spots these emotions in the midst of a growing organization, it may very well be a symptom of changing too quickly or that they didn't time the change well. Growth is good, at an organic pace. My son, Jonathan, did indeed want to grow; he just didn't want to grow all at once. In the same way, organizations should indeed want to grow, but as a by-product of a healthy, natural culture.

WHEN—NOT JUST WHAT

Wise leaders remember that **when** they do something may be as important as **what** they do. Once you know what must be done, you must prepare people for the change emotionally. Then, time it right to insure its success. Leaders must position changes for acceptance. Case in point. For years, Ernest Hamwi had dreamed of creating a waffle that could be eaten as a dessert. But, alas, no one else embraced this idea. Waffles were eaten alone and almost always for breakfast. But at the 1904 World's Fair in St. Louis, Ernest obtained a booth and tried to sell his waffles sprinkled with sugar. Sadly, because July was so hot, few people were willing to try his new waffles. Instead, they were buying ice cream from Arnold, the teenager in the booth next to him... and they were buying them like crazy. Then it happened. The teenager selling ice cream ran out of paper bowls. His customers grew impatient with him as he couldn't wash his ceramic bowls fast enough to reuse them. At that point, Ernest approached Arnold and asked if he could help, by supplying an edible bowl for Arnold's ice cream. Ernest rolled up his waffles into a bowl, and Arnold placed a scoop of ice cream on top. Everyone won. The customers loved them. Arnold kept his sales high, and Ernest finally sold his idea of a waffle dessert. This was the world's very first ice cream cone! Why was 1904 the right time? John Maxwell reminds us that people won't change until they:

- HURT ENOUGH THAT THEY HAVE TO CHANGE

- SEE ENOUGH THAT THEY WANT TO CHANGE

- KNOW ENOUGH THAT THEY ARE ABLE TO CHANGE

Ernest just waited for the right moment for his dream to be realized. Timing is everything.

Depth Not Breadth

Truett Cathy, founder of Chick-fil-A, demonstrated this in a meeting just a few years ago. (I mentioned Chick-fil-A in an earlier chapter.) The executives met to discuss how to expand the number of store units across the U.S. Several of the vice presidents had ideas as to how they could become bigger chicken sandwich distributors—maybe even become number one in the nation! After some time of discussion, Truett Cathy quieted everyone down. He then spoke very deliberately: "I'm tired of talking about getting bigger. I want to talk about getting better. 'Cause if we get better, our customers will make sure we get bigger." Nuff said.

Essentially, Mr. Cathy's "Mark Twain wisdom" boiled down to this. He wanted to improve the culture, knowing that expansion would follow a very healthy culture. Remember: healthy things naturally grow. If you do things organically, (rather than artificially or programmatically), you work on the *depth* of your culture knowing the *breadth* will take care of itself. When a leader wants to grow quickly, he or she often makes program changes, hoping it will make the difference and transform the place. I've found mere *program* changes are temporary and plastic. In contrast, organic changes involve improving the *culture* of an organization. It's like planting seeds in a healthy plot of soil. The growth is authentic, but it doesn't happen quickly. In organizations, this organic change affects how people perceive reality, how they communicate mission, and how they experience community. It's genuine. It looks much more like a little *movement* than a *program*.

Movements Not Programs

Do you know the difference between a movement and a program? Programs are usually launched quickly and with a bang. You've seen it before. An organization promotes a new program—and pulls out all the stops. Billboards, bagels and balloons. But it often doesn't last long. Generally, programs start big, then fizzle and shrink. Soon, the leaders must look for another program. Movements, on the other hand, start very small and grow very large. But it takes time. It's organic. It's like planting seeds in a garden instead of purchasing some artificial flowers. It's the difference between an athlete who uses steroids to build muscle mass, and one who takes the time to eat right, work out and build muscle over time. One is artificial, one is authentic. What's more, not only is the change real, it greatly reduces the growing pains.

A Look at the Book

Check out Mark 4:26-32. In this text, Jesus tells two stories about the Kingdom of God. He said it is like a man who plants seed into the soil and watches the growth. The man's job in the stories is two-fold: he prepares the soil and plants the seed. God's job is to slowly grow the seed into a tree.

1. If the man's job is to prepare the soil and plant the seed, how can we compare this job to ours as leaders who want to grow people?

_____

_____

_____

2. What does it means to create a healthy "environment" in our organization?

_____

_____

_____

3. In verse 27, we read that the plant grew up, but the man didn't even know how. He just planted the seed in good soil, and went to bed each night and got up each day. If God's job is to actually grow the plant in that garden, what does this say to us about not forcing change?

_____

_____

_____

4. How is organic growth a lot like planting a seed in a garden? What role does trust play?

_____

_____

_____

GETTING PERSONAL

Take an honest look at how you try to orchestrate change in your organization. Evaluate your leadership by marking an "X" on the dotted lines below.

|--|

PACE YOUR PEOPLE   RACE YOUR PEOPLE

|--|

EMPHASIS ON "WHEN"   EMPHASIS ON "WHAT"

```
|---------------------------------------------------------------|
  FOCUS ON DEPTH                              FOCUS ON BREADTH


|---------------------------------------------------------------|
  WE STARTED A MOVEMENT                    WE STARTED A PROGRAM
```

1. Discuss your evaluation. Are too many of your "X" marks on the right side of the scale? Why?

_____

_____

_____

2. What action steps should you (or your team) take to monitor the necessary changes?

_____

_____

_____

PRACTICING THE TRUTH

With your team, create a list of the major elements of your organization. These could be divisions, departments, projects, initiatives, or however you divide up your group. Next, list the significant changes within the divisions that have taken place in your organization over the past year.

Discuss: Do you believe you have stayed within the 20 percent change rate we discussed in this chapter? Evaluate these changes. Were they led by about 20 percent of the people? Did you grow too fast or too slow?

Finally, list the most strategic changes that still remain. What are the key changes you still need to make? What are the most important 20 percent of these changes? When should you start?

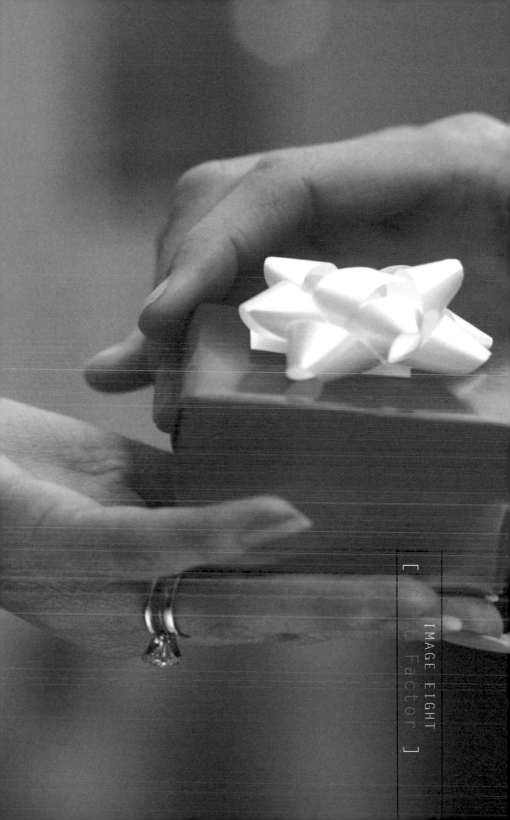

Gift Factor

CULTURES EXPERIENCE CHANGE BASED ON THEIR LEADERS. LEADERS CREATE CHANGE BASED ON THEIR STRENGTHS. A LEADER'S GIFT IS THE PRIMARY WAY HE OR SHE SHAPES THE COMPLEXION OF AN ORGANIZATION.

Years ago, a single man lived alone in an old neighborhood. Because he was very busy with his job, he never took time to upgrade his home. Over the course of fifteen years, the sofa, chairs, and carpet slowly faded. The wallpaper and paintings looked weathered and worn. Even the draperies were sagging. But, alas, the man just didn't care much. He was busy making a living and wasn't concerned with how his house looked. After all, he didn't entertain many guests and he wasn't into appearances.

Then, one year a friend came for a visit on his birthday and gave him a large gift, wrapped up nicely. He could tell this friend had spent some time and money purchasing this gift. When he opened it, he found a beautiful colored-glass vase inside. He'd never seen anything so gorgeous. He placed it on the mantle of the fireplace in his living room and admired it. Without a doubt, it was the best-looking accessory in the whole house. It became his precious possession.

Over time, the man began to ponder how the ornate vase looked out of place in the living room décor. He noticed it was so much nicer than his sofa or chairs, and certainly more exquisite than his dilapidated drapes. One by one, he decided he should replace the other features in the room—the furniture, drapes, carpet, wallpaper and pictures. Within a year, the whole room had dramatically changed. It was stunning!

Hmmm. Isn't it interesting how one little gift could have such an extraordinary effect on an entire room? That vase became a standard for the rest of the furniture—and soon it influenced the old, mediocre surroundings of the living room. In other words, one gift transformed the environment of that man's home. Wise leaders follow the analogy in this story. First, leaders must look at their culture with fresh eyes and see the need for change, just like that man. (Sometimes, we become blind to the needed changes in our culture.)

Second, they must allow their gift to instruct them as to how they'll best bring about change in the organization. Generally, a leader's primary gift will become the chief instrument in orchestrating change within a team. The gift will lead the way. Put another way, organizational cultures experience transformation based on the strengths of the leader. Some leaders attack the need for change through their word gifts—they will motivate or teach or equip their teams with their words. Other leaders will do it via their organization skills—they will restructure the teams. Still others will do it through their strategic thinking and planning skills. In any case, it will come about as leaders play to their strengths. That's why no two leaders may orchestrate change exactly alike. They have to find their "style" on how to initiate the renovation. The "gift" of the chief influencer will be the primary means to bring about change.

For example, Ford Motor Company has gone through some rough times over the last few years. Between 1999 and 2006, they were led by three different CEOs: Jacques Nasser, Bill Ford, Jr., and Alan Mulally. Each of these men took the chief executive position knowing they would need to make some changes to salvage the market share Ford had in the automobile industry. However, each man had a different "gift" and went about making the changes in a uniquely different manner. Mr. Nasser was a rough, tough, "bottom-line" leader. His nickname is "The Axe." Upon his promotion, he immediately cut staff, cut costs, and bought new auto companies like Volvo, and the Range Rover from BMW. He has a bias for action. He was known as a cut-throat, do-whatever-it-takes kind of leader. Unfortunately, his financial decisions were fast but not accurate. In 2001, Ford Motor Company lost $5.5 billion. In October, Mr. Nasser was replaced by Ford's Chairman, Bill Ford, Jr. (the grandson of Henry Ford). Bill went about making changes very differently. He was much more caring in his approach. He was more of a "responder" to the culture. As an environmentalist, he looked to develop ways to produce more fuel efficient cars and trucks. Relationships with his team were important. In fact, when the Ford Rouge Powerhouse plant exploded in 1999, Bill Ford insisted in visiting the site. When one of his staff warned him, "Generals don't visit the front lines," he responded, "Then bust me down to private."

Unfortunately, Bill Ford's gifts weren't enough to lead his company out of a sinking market share. So, in 2005 he was replaced by Alan Mulally, a former executive with the Boeing Company. Alan is more of an engineer-type of leader. He played a role in the design and production of several Boeing jets during his time with them.[1] So, his style is more of a "thinking and processing" method for bringing about change. In each case, however—Jacques, Bill or Alan—we see a leader changing the organization in their own way. There isn't one right way to orchestrate change.

You will find this true for you as well. Don't become discouraged when you see another leader doing things differently than you would. We often feel uncomfortable emulating some other leader who pulls off an incredible change.

We shouldn't. Always learn from other great leaders, but don't copy their style, especially if your gifts are different. Lead from your strengths. In your primary gift area, you will be most:

- INTUITIVE
- COMFORTABLE
- NATURAL

- PASSIONATE
- PRODUCTIVE
- INFLUENTIAL

In 1983, I took over the college department at a church in San Diego. I followed a very gifted leader named Jim. Jim was talented musically, relationally, artistically, and he had a witty sense of humor. As a result, the culture was very artsy and musical. It was intimidating to follow his leadership style. I knew I couldn't try to shape the culture the way Jim did. It wouldn't be natural, and I would only become frustrated. So, I figured out what my strength was. I would be an equipper. I would train students to lead and to impact their campuses all across San Diego. Furthermore, we identified the strengths within the college department. In the end, this is what saved me. In seven years, we grew 1,000 percent. We did it through the gifts we possessed, not by imitating the pattern of the former leader's unique gifts.

You may remember the story of James Braddock. In 2005, his story was told in a movie called *Cinderella Man*. What I love about Jim is that he wanted to help his country during the Great Depression in the 1930s. Driven by love and this vision, he returned to boxing (after breaking his hand and losing almost every dime he had) and took on a contender in the boxing ring. Braddock, a retired boxer, had become an ordinary shipping-dock worker, but he began to carry "the hopes and dreams of the disenfranchised on his shoulders."[2] His amazing comeback to fight and beat the champion became a source of inspiration to so many hopeless people in that era. The bottom line? Jim hoped to change a hopeless culture. He wasn't a CEO or a strategist. He was a boxer. So he took his gift into the boxing ring... and changed America.

Does this *Habitude* apply to anyone? You tell me. In 1921, Lewis Lawes became the warden at Sing Sing Prison. No prison was tougher than Sing Sing during that time. But when Lawes retired some twenty years later, the prison had become a humanitarian institution. Those who studied the system said the credit for this change belonged to Lawes. But when he was asked about the transformation, he said, "I owe it all to my wonderful wife, Catherine."

Catherine Lawes was a young mother with three children when her husband became the warden. Everyone warned her to never step foot inside the prison, but that didn't stop Catherine. When the first prison basketball game was held, she attended with her three young kids and sat in the stands with the inmates. She insisted on getting to know them and their records. She discovered one convicted murderer was blind so she paid him a visit. Holding his hand in hers she said, "Do you read Braille?" "What's Braille?" he asked.

Over the next several months she taught him how to read. Years later he would weep out of love for her. Later, Catherine found a deaf-mute in prison. She went to school to learn how to use sign language so they could talk. Many said that Catherine was like having Jesus visiting Sing Sing prison, from 1921 to 1937.

She was killed suddenly in a car accident in 1937. When the prisoners didn't see her or Lewis the next day, they all knew something was wrong. The following day, her body was resting in a casket in her home, nearly a mile from the prison. The prison staff was shocked to see a large crowd of the toughest, hardened criminals gathered like a herd of animals at the prison gate. The staff reported tears streaming down their cheeks. Remarkably, the prison guards decided to let them attend her memorial service, without supervision, as long as they checked back in later that night. The prison gates opened and that group of inmates walked to her home to pay their respects to Catherine, a woman who changed the culture of Sing Sing. What's more, every one of them returned to the prison that night.[3] Extraordinary. If Catherine were here today, she'd say she wasn't anyone special. She just used the gifts she had and transformed that prison. What's your gift?

A Look at the Book

1. Check out Proverbs 22:29. The passage talks about what "skills" can do for someone. How does this passage fit into this *Habitude*?

_____

_____

_____

2. Proverbs 18:16 says that a "man's gift makes room for him and brings him before great people." This text is similar to the one above. Have you seen your primary gift make room for you and help you accomplish a goal? How?

_____

_____

_____

3. One of the most popular stories in the Old Testament is the account of David facing Goliath, found in 1 Samuel 17. As you read this chapter, notice how everyone assumed David had no chance facing the giant. What's more, when he insisted on fighting Goliath, King Saul assumed he would wear his armor and fight his way. Instead, David chose to use five smooth stones. Jot down some thoughts on how this story illustrates "The Gift Factor" in this young leader's life.

_____

_____

_____

GETTING PERSONAL

Take a few moments and evaluate your own leadership. Mark where you have failed to approach the need to change your culture because you didn't capitalize on your primary gifts and style.

1. Reflect on a time your team or organization was failing to reach a goal. How did you respond?

    _____ You didn't speak up at all.

    _____ You brought up the issue, but you deferred to others for the solution.

    _____ You acted, but you imitated a style you'd seen in the past.

    _____ You discussed it, then led according to your primary gifts and style.

2. When it comes to changing your organizational culture, what's your normal course of action?

_____

_____

_____

PRACTICING THE TRUTH

Have you identified your primary gift as a leader? If not, check out the Growing Leaders website (www.GrowingLeaders.com) and study the resources: "Trombone Player Wanted" or "A Life of Influence" or "The Life You Were Meant to Live." If you do know your primary gift, examine your city and find a leader who has changed their organization's culture and has a similar primary gift. Interview them and seek to learn how you can bring about change using your style.

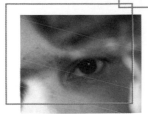

Science Class

COLLEGE SCIENCE CLASS HAS TWO ELEMENTS: LECTURE AND LAB. MOST
ORGANIZATIONS ARE STRONG IN LECTURE, BUT WEAK IN LAB. A LAB IS A SAFE
PLACE FOR STUDENTS TO EXPERIMENT IN LEADERSHIP. THEY NEED EXPERIENCE.

I remember enrolling in my first college science course, prior to my freshman year of college. I entered with a little bit of fear and trepidation. Everyone told me it was a three-credit course, yet those same people added, "But it's a little different than your typical three-credit course." I soon found out what they meant. Students had to spend much more than three hours a week in the course. It required attending a "lecture" on Monday, Wednesday and Fridays, then participating in a "lab." I only had a vague idea about what a lab was. It was a place where I would invest two extra hours each week, experimenting with the information I received from the textbook, during the lecture. Often, I spent six hours a week on that three-credit course, attempting to figure out what that textbook meant!

One afternoon, after reading about a flammable liquid in chapter seven of our text, I entered the lab with my partner and confessed, "I have no idea what this book is trying to say."

"Did you study the chapter?" my lab partner inquired.

"Yes, but those words didn't make any sense. I can't remember the elements in the gases or the liquids in this chapter, and I have no idea what makes it so flammable."

The two of us proceeded to do the corresponding experiment, coupling the liquid with other kinds of liquids and gases. What ensued next can only be described as hilarious. My partner and I deposited two drops of the liquid we'd been reading about into a test tube, which sat on a Bunsen burner. All at once, it bubbled. We stepped back... then, BOOM! The liquid spayed all over the ceiling and everywhere else within about ten feet. It was a chemical reaction. Everything was covered, from counter to ceiling, with a new liquid we'd just created by joining two compounds together.

After taking a moment to make sure both of us were OK, the lab attendant and the two of us laughed until we hurt. It was like a scene out of the Disney movie, *Flubber*.

Needless to say, I never forgot that little experiment. Furthermore, I learned what that liquid was and what made it so flammable. I got an "A" on the next test. The reason is simple. What I had failed to learn merely reading a textbook, I grasped experientially through participating in a lab. This is why science must always be taught through both a lecture and a lab. Sometimes, students like me just don't get it without first-hand experience—even if it turns out to be a comedy!

Let's apply this little lesson. In order to become a training organization—one that reproduces leaders and experiences a transformational culture—you must understand that your workplace operates like a college science class. There are two components: lecture and lab. There are words that top leaders speak, which doubtless are important. However, your environment must also include a "lab" for them to experiment with the changes you desire. There must be instruction and experimentation. Principles and practice.

Consider what a laboratory is. A "lab" is simply a safe place in which to experiment. Once a student has read the text book, the lab provides a place for students to participate and try out their book knowledge. Even in my messy experiment, it was a relatively safe place where the students were being watched, coached and evaluated. But, we were the participants. Sometimes, I get the feeling that business offices, school campuses and churches are strong on "lecture" and weak on "lab." We don't really furnish safe places for training and experimentation, so it isn't safe for students to fail. This is why so few actually practice what you preach to them—it's less risky to sit and watch and clap for the lecture.

It seems most organizations—even most school campuses—suffer from the "Football Problem." Do you know what the "Football Problem" is? Have you ever been to a football game? There are always two major components. One—there are 22 people running around on the field in desperate need of rest. Two—there are 50,000 people in the stands in desperate need of exercise! This is a picture of many organizations: a few people do all the work; the rest watch. Unfortunately, the people watching never improve and never really own the vision.

According to the periodical *Worthwhile* (March 2005) 75 percent of today's employees will need training or development just to keep the jobs they have today. Only 20 percent of the workforce has the skills that half of tomorrow's jobs will require. And most of these people learn through hands-on experience. Consider this discovery:

- 67% LEARN WHEN WORKING WITH A COLLEAGUE ON A TASK.

- 21% LEARN WHILE DOING THEIR OWN RESEARCH.

- 10% LEARN FROM A COLLEAGUE EXPLAINING SOMETHING PERSONALLY.

- 2% LEARN THROUGH MANUALS OR TEXTBOOKS.

These statistics are probably not a news flash to you. People need a lab in order to grow. With first-hand training experience, a culture takes shape more quickly and solidly. *Information plus participation equals transformation.* Just ask the folks at the Disney Company and Pixar Animation Studios. When Disney CEO Bob Iger and Pixar Chairman Steve Jobs met to discuss partnership, the results were astounding. Steve Jobs agreed to sell Pixar outright to Disney—but in return, Disney allowed Pixar to take over their animation studios.[1] Wow. It's as if Nemo has swallowed the whale. Disney recognized that Pixar had much to teach them about 21st century animation. By providing a safe "lab" to Pixar, it would propel them into indisputable leadership of this industry. Today, these two magnificent companies have formed one big "lab" to experiment and grow.

My friend, Dwayne Carson, has developed this kind of "lab" at Liberty University in Virginia. Dwayne loves to create safe environments where students can learn to lead. So, he's developed a "farm system" on campus, where students can begin leading from day one. I mentioned this idea in the "Joshua Problem." Just as "pro" baseball has Single A, Double A, and Triple A leagues for young players to prepare for the Majors, Liberty has places for students to "play" at suitable levels. Incoming freshmen are challenged to become prayer group leaders. It is an entry-level position where first year students get valuable experience and add value to their residence hall. In their second year, he has a Double A opportunity where they can lead discipleship or growth groups.

The third year, many students take leadership positions like RA, SGA or club leaders. Finally, during their senior year there are advanced (Major League) positions to continue stretching them as leaders preparing for the outside world. If you ask Dwayne his secret, he'd likely tell you he's set up a science class for leaders—with both a lecture and lab. And this "science class" has helped transform the leadership culture on that campus.

EVENTS AND PROCESS

For years I've believed that real change happens in students when leaders use both "events" and "process" to foster that life change. Events might be conferences, retreats, concerts, seminars or youth camps. They are one time meetings that spark the need for change. At events, new ideas enter the minds of those who attend. However, most people need a "process" to follow the event to cause real life-change to occur. A "process" involves the weeks that follow the event, where attendees meet together to discuss and apply the ideas discussed at the event. They are communities, or mentoring relationships or accountability partnerships that follow up on the ideas and insure that they become a habit in the lives of those who came to the event.

Notice the following columns that describe the role of each one:

EVENTS	PROCESS
1. Encourage decisions	1. Encourages development
2. Motivate people	2. Matures people
3. Are a calendar issue	3. Is a consistency issue
4. Usually about a big group	4. Usually about a small group
5. Challenge people	5. Changes people
6. Become a catalyst	6. Becomes a culture
7. Easy	7. Difficult

Events are like the "lecture" and process is like the "lab." We need both, but we must get beyond the glitz and glamour of merely holding events and begin to work on the process—which is what really changes people.

A LOOK AT THE BOOK

1. Jesus trained His twelve disciples using both "lectures" and "labs." He verbally taught them, and He furnished first-hand experiences for those emerging leaders to practice what He taught. Read Matthew 9:35 – Matthew 10:42. Jot down how Jesus used these two ingredients to train his men:

LECTURE	LAB

2. Why do you think most organizations are stronger in providing "lectures" than "labs?"

_____

_____

_____

3. Can you name a time when someone trained you to do something using both a lecture and a lab?

_____

_____

_____

GETTING PERSONAL

Reflect and respond to these evaluation questions below:

1. Where are your "safe places" that allow potential leaders to experiment in leadership?

_____

_____

_____

2. What places in your organization still lack "labs" that prepare potential leaders for service?

_____

_____

_____

3. List below the three most important departments in your organization. Now, list how these departments utilize "lectures" and "labs" to prepare potential leaders for positions:

DEPARTMENT	LECTURE	LAB
1._____	1._____	1._____
2._____	2._____	2._____
3._____	3._____	3._____

PRACTICING THE TRUTH

Identify the places where your organization is weak, either in lecture or lab, as you provide training to potential leaders. List them on paper. Now, come up with a list of three creative ideas for how you could furnish what's missing to those potential leaders. Discuss with your team how you could add these lectures and labs as you prepare the people on your team.

IMAGE TEN

[The Ripple Effect]

The Ripple Effect

CULTURES EMERGE FROM LIFE-CHANGING ENVIRONMENTS. ENVIRONMENTS EMERGE FROM SMALL COMMUNITIES THAT FOSTER DISCOVERY AND SELF-DISCLOSURE. CREATE COMMUNITIES AND ENVIRONMENTS. CULTURE FOLLOWS.

Everyone has thrown a small rock into a pond or a lake, and watched the effect it has when it hits. When that little stone hits the surface, it makes a splash. Following that splash is a ripple effect. Starting with one small ring of water, new rings begin to spread outward in concentric circles. With a big enough splash, those rings can continue for several minutes expanding out into the calm waters surrounding the starting point.

Growing up, my family used to visit Lake Harrington in Kentucky every summer. I could spend hours throwing rocks into that lake, skimming them on the water's surface or trying to hit certain locations in the lake. My favorite memory from these moments was causing a ripple effect. I would throw a rock as far out into the water as I could, then watch to see if the circles of waves could return all the way to the banks of the lake where I stood. With a big enough rock and some calm water, it was amazing how that ripple effect could go on and on.

Organizations experience ripple effects too—both good and bad ones. It's the effect of small decisions on the culture of an ordinarily calm team or department. Those decisions are like rocks hitting the surface that cause an expanded effect into the atmosphere of the organization. For instance, George Kelling caused a wonderful ripple effect on the culture of New York City in the early 1990s. He was asked to study the rising crime rate that worsened each year within the five boroughs of the city. Violent crimes, rapes, murders and drug traffic were soaring. At least until George Kelling threw a rock into the water there. After studying a high-crime neighborhood, he came back to the city officials with a suggestion: "The windows are all broken in that neighborhood. Instead of spending millions on new police officers, let's fix the windows and see what happens."

Almost immediately after replacing the windows and repainting the frames, crime and drug deals dropped more than 60 percent. This brought families out to their front porches again. People stayed outside and talked, even after dark. Vendors began to venture back into the area. This "crowd" further impacted the drug dealers. It forced almost every one of them to leave. George Kelling's decision was based on his "Broken Windows Theory." He said later that when windows are broken, it suggests to criminals that no one is watching and no one cares. When you replace the windows and paint the sills, it tells everyone that even the small things are being watched.[1] His little theory had a ripple effect on the neighborhood. Crime rates went from extremely high to almost nothing. That's quite a splash.

ENVIRONMENTS AND COMMUNITIES

So, if even small decisions can have a ripple effect on a culture, what decisions are most important to a leader if they're to positively influence that culture? In other words, how do we find the biggest rock that will make the biggest splash and cause the widest ripple? How do we know which windows to fix, so we can affect the culture in our neighborhood?

Put simply, leaders don't directly change the culture. They do it indirectly through small groups of people. Wise leaders know they cannot simply declare a culture change—any more than George Kelling could just announce that criminals and drug dealers must leave the neighborhood. No, he fixed some windows that led to the departure of those criminals. In the same way, leaders create healthy communities within an organization—communities that experience authentic relationships filled with self-disclosure and discovery. Healthy communities are the "windows" leaders fix in order to affect change. From these authentic communities, positive environments emerge. And those environments lead to a change in culture. Keep in mind—there are as many micro-cultures as there are leaders.

It would be difficult to overestimate the power of small communities. Consider this statement: there is no life change without life exchange. When people really exchange life together, they become real and begin operating in a more healthy and productive manner. Like a ripple effect created by a rock in the water, all cultures begin change from small groups of people that spread outward. So, the rings in the water of your organization flow outward in this order:

- COMMUNITIES: Clusters of people in relationship with one another, working toward a goal.

- ENVIRONMENTS: The combination of many of those communities affecting the whole.

- CULTURE: The result of healthy environments on the pathos and ethos of an organization.

Case in point is the U.S.S. Benfold and Captain Michael Abrashoff. Under Captain Abrashoff, the culture on that Navy ship was radically transformed in six months. He did it by creating working communities based on crew-members sharing similar strengths and purpose, instead of rank. It wasn't about a chain of command but a chain of communities. He placed privates, lieutenants and sergeants on teams and gave them responsibility to solve problems. These communities were rewarded as they brought results, and this created a revolutionary environment in each department on board that ship. Discipline could be handled differently and money was actually returned to the government because jobs got done more efficiently. In the end, everyone loved the culture that emerged. On average, only 54 percent of U.S. sailors remain in the Navy after their second tour of duty. Due to the culture Captain Abrashoff established, 100 percent of the U.S.S. Benfold's career sailors signed on for an additional tour. The result: Abrashoff saved the Navy $1.6 million in personnel-related costs in 1998. How did he accomplish this? Through communities and environments that created a unique culture on his ship. It's the ripple effect.

One of my heroes is Charles Simeon. Simeon had a ripple effect on the Anglican Church during the 19th century in the U.K. When he got discouraged at the unhealthy culture of the churches in England, a mentor suggested he take a parish across the street from Cambridge University. He began to focus on preparing young men for the ministry—so he could change the culture of his church movement. What happened was nothing short of amazing. First, he signed up to speak in chapel as often as possible. Following those chapel services, he would invite interested students to a "Conversation Group" on Tuesday nights, where he would go deeper in his teaching. At those groups he would hand-pick sharp young leaders to participate in a Supper Club at his home on Sunday nights. There, he would equip about 12 to 15 leaders for ministry. Within that club, he would zero in on about three or four seniors who were preparing to graduate. They were his inner circle.

SIMEON'S CONCENTRIC CIRCLES

Each of his meetings represented a new community, with a deeper level of commitment and purpose. As his students finished school, he would try to place them in parishes across the country. He did this quite successfully... for 54 years.

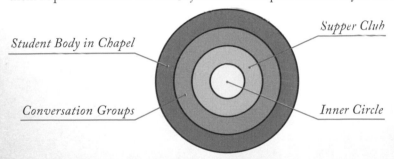

Student Body in Chapel

Supper Club

Conversation Groups

Inner Circle

By the time of his death, one third of all the Anglican churches were led by those he had trained.[2] Talk about a ripple effect.

A Look at the Book

The ripple effect is occurring almost every day of our lives. Each decision we make, has some corresponding effect on others. Check out the passages below which illustrate this truth in the lives of two leaders.

1. Samson made a decision which had a negative ripple effect. Read Judges 16. Jot down what his decision was. How did it have an impact on the nation of Israel?

_____

_____

_____

2. Solomon made a decision that had a positive ripple effect. Read 1 Kings 3. Jot down what his decision was. How did it have an impact on the nation of Israel?

_____

_____

_____

3. Check out Exodus 18. In this passage, Moses was the sole leader in Israel who did everything himself. His father-in-law, Jethro, confronted him on this decision and challenged him to build communities of leaders around him to help him lead and make decisions for Israel. Read verse 23 and summarize how Moses' decision would ripple positively throughout the population.

_____

_____

_____

4. In what ways did the leadership communities affect the culture in Israel? (Exodus 18:24-27).

_____

_____

_____

GETTING PERSONAL

Take a moment and evaluate the ripple effect of your decisions. Write out your honest answer.

1. Name the last time you made a leadership decision that negatively affected others. How?

_____

_____

_____

2. Name the last time you made a leadership decision that positively affected others. How?

_____

_____

_____

3. How have you capitalized on creating communities to foster an environment, to create a culture?

_____

_____

_____

PRACTICING THE TRUTH

Meet with your team and brainstorm the kinds of environments you wish to create in your organization. Discuss how you'll create them. How will forming small communities help? If you form them, what will be the purpose of those communities? Finally, do some creative thinking on how the communities will feed the environment which will impact the culture you desire. Discuss.

Cathedral Building

MOST BUILDERS SEE ONLY THE PAYCHECK, OR THE TASK IN FRONT OF THEM. GREAT BUILDERS SEE THE BIG PICTURE: THEY'RE BUILDING A CATHEDRAL. LEADERS MAINTAIN A PERSPECTIVE BEYOND THEIR OWN LIMITED VISION AND CHANGE THE CULTURE.

A man strolled along a downtown street one day. He enjoyed all the hustle and bustle of the city, filled with street vendors during the day, and bright lights in the evening. He loved the sounds of the streets, the sights of the advertisements everywhere, the feel of people moving about, and the taste of the hot pretzels he munched on as he walked to his apartment. He even liked the smell of the downtown area where he worked. It carried the feeling of growth and change and progress.

This particular day, he decided to walk a different route home, and he noticed a new structure going up along the street. From the work done so far, he could tell it promised to be a large building, very ornate and probably quite important. He got curious, so he decided to inquire what kind of building was going up. He walked up to a construction worker and asked what he was doing. Without even looking up, the builder replied, "I'm laying bricks, what does it look like?"

Obviously, this wasn't the answer this man was looking for, so he located a second worker and approached him with the same question. The worker grunted, obviously in a bad mood. "Hmph. I'm drawing a paycheck."

This still wasn't the answer the man was seeking, so he thought he'd give it one more try. He tapped a third construction worker on the shoulder and asked the same question, "What are you doing?" This time, he got the answer he was looking for. The builder looked up toward the sky and with a gleam in his eye, he responded: "I'm building a cathedral!"[1]

There's a lesson in this little story for leaders. Consider these three construction workers. None of them were lying when they responded to the question, "What are you doing?" However, the first one only perceived his work from a logistical perspective. He only saw what he was doing personally. The second could only see his work from a tactical viewpoint.

The outcome of his work was a paycheck—which was the only reason he showed up for work! The third worker, however, was able to see the big picture, and how his personal effort was part of something bigger than he was.

These three perspectives are central to understanding culture. I use military terms to describe them. Let me define these terms, so you can evaluate how folks are motivated on your team:

1. LOGISTICAL
   This is the "here and now" perspective. I only see what's in front of me today.

2. TACTICAL
   This perspective is broader and futuristic, but is still limited to my world.

3. STRATEGIC
   This is the big picture perspective that enables me to see how everything fits into the overall plan.

When leaders can move people beyond their own personal tasks to see the big picture, it not only helps to align everyone's work, it accelerates the creation of a desired culture. Part of the key to building a culture stems from the leader's ability to communicate clear vision for how every team member fits into the plan. It also diminishes a "primadona attitude" or selfish, territorial behavior. It enables team members to help each other, because they think outside of their own "box." All cultures require someone to maintain the big picture and to move others toward the big picture.

When leaders fail to provide perspective, people will likely act in their own interests. Just ask Earl Weaver. Earl was the manager of the Baltimore Orioles baseball team more than thirty years ago. One of his bright young stars was Reggie Jackson. Reggie reached first base one night and desperately wanted to steal second. He knew he could do it against the opposing pitcher, but Earl Weaver never gave him the signal to steal. Earl had set a rule that no one was to steal a base without his signal. Reggie was fuming because his manager obviously didn't recognize how fast he was. Finally, he decided to steal without a signal. He got a good jump and sped toward second base, sliding in…safe! He got up and brushed the dirt off his uniform, feeling justified for making the decision on his own. Now everyone saw how fast he was.

When the inning was over, Earl motioned for Reggie to come over and talk. When they met, Earl said, "Reggie, I knew you were fast enough to steal off of that pitcher. I didn't give you the signal for two reasons. First, if you stole second, you'd open up first base, allowing our opposition to intentionally walk Lee May, our best power-hitter besides you. When they did just that, it took the bat right out of his hands. Second, our next hitter wasn't doing well against their pitcher, forcing me to use a pinch hitter to move runners up.

This ruined my plans for using him at a different spot later in the game." Earl paused, then finished. "Reggie—remember that you see the game from your own angle, but I see the big picture. Next time, wait for my signal."

In 2002, the Anaheim Angels surprised everyone and won the World Series. Manager Mike Soscia said later that it was all about creating a new culture on the team. He didn't have any big names on the team, but he knew if they could forget their personal stats for a season and play as a team, they could go all the way. Mike began casting vision for the big picture to his players in February. Next, he began to reward players who moved runners up on base, and penalized hitters who failed to do it. Beginning in April, he posted team results on how well his guys were playing rather than personal statistics. He only had to do this for one month. The culture began to change. That year, with no big superstars, the Angels won the World Series. Why? Because some free agents and average players got together and acted on the big picture. While talent is important, playing as a team is far more important to winning championships. Individuals win trophies but teams win championships.

This is the job of leadership—moving people from logistical to tactical to strategic thinking. Providing every team member a perspective that empowers them to act unselfishly; to use their talent for something bigger than themselves, and to see how even a little job contributes toward a very important mission. Leaders who contagiously spread this vision change their organizational culture.

In 1961, President John F. Kennedy did the unthinkable. In a speech, he cast vision for putting a man on the moon before the end of the decade. The story's been told over and over, but at the time he cast this vision, the U.S. didn't even have the technology to do it. However, his big picture perspective was infectious. Immediately, the team at NASA focused their energies on this monumental mission. Staff members who for years "felt like a piece of furniture," began to display unusual performance—all because of this vision. It turned average workers into extraordinary workers. To this day, NASA has this revolutionary performance leap on record.

A year after President Kennedy cast the moon-landing vision, he visited NASA to check on their progress. As he walked the halls, he ventured into a small room accidentally. Everyone in his entourage followed him; after all, he was the president. When he entered the room, he saw a custodian with a broom. He reached out to shake his hand and asked what his job was. The custodian paused, then smiled and replied, "I'm putting a man on the moon, Mr. President."

I love it. The custodian got it. Sounds like a cathedral builder to me.

A Look at the Book

Check out 2 Kings 3:5-18. This passage tells the story of the King of Israel and his battle against the King of Moab. He rallied two allies and marched across the desert to fight the Moabites. Sadly, their troops ran out of water along the way. Israel's king all but gave up the entire vision.

1. When they decided to approach the prophet Elisha, they begged him for water. Notice how they had their eyes on the "water" not the "war." How does facing a challenge distract people from the big picture goals they've set?

_____

_____

_____

2. Elisha's response was classic. He told the kings that God would grant them water, but that this was a "small thing in the sight of the Lord. He will also give the Moabites into their hands (verse 18)." They asked for the logistical goal not the strategic goal; they focused on the water not the war. They saw only the immediate need not the big picture need. Name a time this has happened to you.

_____

_____

_____

3. Jesus demonstrates a big picture perspective in two passages. Jot down your response to them:

   a. John 12:27-28. Jesus refuses to focus on the logistical need for safety.

_____

_____

_____

   b. Matthew 9:36-38. Jesus looks at the multitudes, but sees something different.

_____

_____

_____

4. Are you a naturally "big picture" person or a "detail" person? How does this affect your actions?

_____

_____

_____

GETTING PERSONAL

Evaluate how well you embrace and pass on a big picture perspective. How do you see your job?

1. LOGISTICAL
   What's your immediate job in front of you now?

_____

_____

2. TACTICAL
   What's your departmental job this year?

_____

_____

3. STRATEGIC
   What's the ultimate job or mission, over the long haul?

_____

_____

PRACTICING THE TRUTH

The next time you meet with your team, take a moment and ask them what their job is. Then, ask them what the mission is for your organization. Finally, ask them how their job fits into the big picture mission of your organization. See if you get any surprises. Discuss what your team members said.

IMAGE TWELVE
[Dorothy's Way]

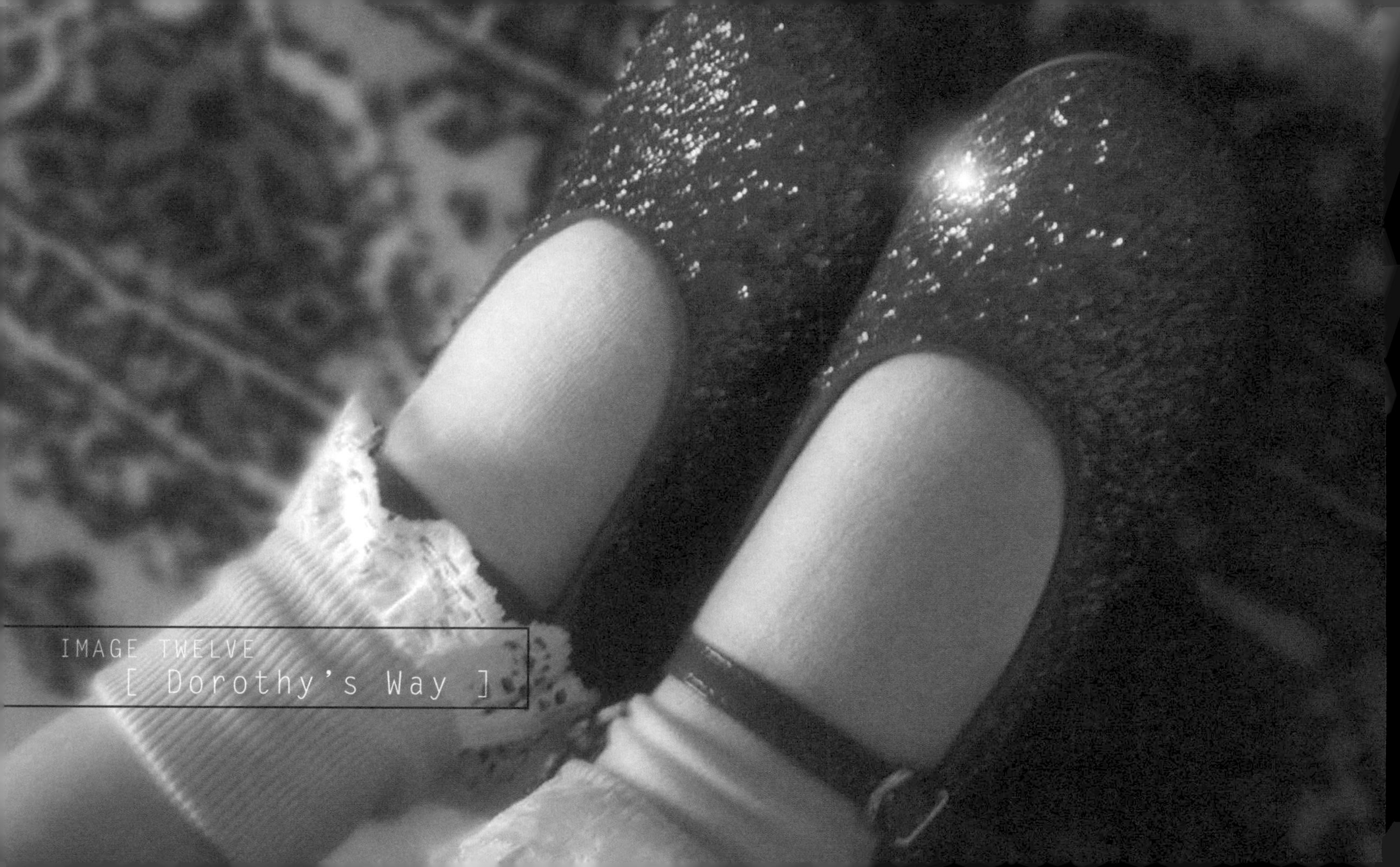

IMAGE TWELVE

[Dorothy's Way]

Dorothy's Way

IN THE CLASSIC STORY OF "THE WIZARD OF OZ," DOROTHY ILLUSTRATES A NEW KIND OF LEADER. SHE INVITES HER FRIENDS ON A JOURNEY, HELPS THEM DISCOVER THEIR GIFTS, ENCOURAGES THEM, AND WALKS WITH THEM RATHER THAN INSISTING ON BEING UP FRONT. SHE DOESN'T HAVE ALL THE ANSWERS BUT SHE GETS THEM TO THEIR GOAL.

One of my favorite memories as a kid was watching the movie *The Wizard of Oz* on television. It came on every year. We would pop popcorn and sit around as a family watching Dorothy, the scarecrow, the tin man, and the cowardly lion leave the munchkins in the Land of Oz and make their way to the Emerald City. I still enjoy the movie. It's a classic.

Today, however, I watch it through a different lens. I sat with my own kids a few years ago and learned all kinds of new things from Dorothy—as I watched the film from a leadership perspective. (I know it sounds crazy, but I seem to find leadership principles in almost every movie I see, including *Dumb and Dumber* and *Napoleon Dynamite*!) This time, my leadership discovery came from a very ordinary girl from Kansas who would not claim to be a leader at all.

As I observe trends in our culture, it seems to me that there is a cry for a new kind of leader today. We have moved through various leadership styles over the last fifty years, and many of them can be seen in this classic movie. Reflect on the characters in the movie for a moment and note the three kinds of leaders in it:

1. THE WICKED WITCH OF THE WEST
   She has her cronies, but they follow because she forces them to do so. She leads from manipulation or coercion. In fact, when she melts, her followers celebrate.

2. THE WIZARD OF OZ
   He is the all-powerful leader who leads through intimidation and superiority. He is all-wise and all-powerful—the kind of leader we all tend to imagine is the best one for the job.

3. Dorothy

> She is an unlikely leader who doesn't have all the answers, but invites her friends on a journey, helps them discover their gifts, and walks with them rather than insisting on being up front.

At first glance, Dorothy appears all wrong as a model of leadership. I am certain she never felt like she was a leader. She doesn't fit the gender stereotype, and she's quite young. Instead of being a person who has all the solutions and knows exactly what to do next—she is herself on a journey, a seeker, often bewildered and vulnerable. Yet she is determined to get her team—made up of a scarecrow, a tin man, and a cowardly lion—to the wizard, where they can find what they're looking for. Armed with this resolve, she walks down the yellow brick road on a journey of discovery with her new-found friends. No one expects her to have all the answers. They don't want a "sage on the stage," but a "guide on the side" to help them reach their goal.

Let's contrast Dorothy with the Great Wizard himself. Frequently, many of us avoid leadership positions because we hold an image of a leader in our heads that looks much like the Wizard of Oz. Remember how he introduces himself? He says, "I am Oz, the great and powerful!" In other words—just look to me for any answers you need. I am in charge. Because few of us believe we're really this good, we conclude we must not be a leader. But, do you remember what happens in the end? Little Toto (Dorothy's dog) pulls back the curtain to reveal that the Great Wizard is a rather normal guy hiding behind an imposing image. This all-powerful leader was, in a sense, exposed as a fraud. He wasn't a Superman or a Lone Ranger after all. It's all a front.

When you think of Dorothy, the picture is so different. She introduces herself to the Wizard as "Dorothy, the small and meek." Instead of sitting confident in a control booth, she's stuck in a predicament—still a little frazzled from the tornado, far from home, needing to find the way. As she begins her journey to the Emerald City, she finds other needy characters (the scarecrow, the tin man, and the lion) and her earnestness, her compassion, and her spark of determination galvanizes them into a team. She ends up revealing that they each had the brains, the heart, and the courage they were seeking already inside of them. Dorothy doesn't have the knowledge to help them avoid all the pitfalls or dangers. She doesn't protect them from all the threats—but she encourages them, and she doesn't give up. Her passion holds strong and fosters the same resolve in each of her team members. Dorothy has so invested in them that the lion, the scarecrow, and the tin man all decide they will get to the Wizard to help Dorothy—even if they didn't get what they wanted! Now that's loyalty.

This is a picture of a new kind of leader for our culture today. It was a team effort and no one person was the only star. Each one stood up for the others before it was over. Each one had gifts and abilities. Dorothy simply ran point.

Management guru Peter Drucker notes that these "next generation leaders" must be okay with not having all the answers. They must be humble enough to seek wisdom from others, yet courageous enough to act when it's time. Drucker suggests that "the leader of the past was a person who knew how to tell. The leader of the future will be a person who knows how to ask." They are marked by these qualities:

1. HIGHLY RELATIONAL

2. INTERPRET CULTURE WELL

3. EMOTIONALLY SECURE

4. SHARE OWNERSHIP FREELY

5. EMPOWER OTHERS

6. COMFORTABLE WITH UNCERTAINTY

7. LISTEN AND FOSTER SELF-DISCOVERY

8. EMBRACE THE ROLE OF A MENTOR

9. LESS FORMAL IN STRUCTURE

10. DRIVEN BY SERVICE MORE THAN EGO

I believe I see these Dorothy-type leaders in more and more places. Truett Cathy and his executive team at Chick-fil-A restaurants demonstrate this humble, learning, serving style. They're closed on Sundays so their employees can spend time with their families in worship. They serve in teams and seek wisdom from those they serve in order to continue to be a learning organization. They are all about adding value to their communities, not just selling chicken. David Salyers, their Vice President of Marketing, told me he went on a trip with Dan Cathy, who leads Chick-fil-A. When they arrived at their hotel, David realized his shirts had gotten wrinkled in his luggage. He told Dan he wished someone would invent luggage that wouldn't wrinkle shirts! When he awoke in the morning, he saw that Dan Cathy had gotten up early and had ironed all of his shirts.

Captain Michael Abrashoff led the worst performing ship in the Pacific Ocean, the U.S.S. *Benfold.* In six months he transformed it into the best performing ship in the Pacific. How'd he do it? Dorothy's Way. He interviewed all his sailors and got to know their strengths. He formed teams that became task forces to solve problems in the area of their strengths. When they did, the entire crew got to celebrate. Within months, sailors requested to stay under his leadership. He shared ownership of that ship's problems and solutions and found he had capable men and women who could lead. One day he walked the deck, observing his sailors painting the ship. (They did this numerous times each year because the bolts would rust.) He asked one of the sailors how it was going. The sailor responded, "Permission to be honest, sir?" The captain motioned for the sailor to come talk to him.

In that conversation the sailor simply asked, "Sir, has the Navy ever heard of stainless steel?" The rest is history. Abrashoff commissioned that sailor to head up a task team to find a way to replace the old bolts with stainless steel bolts. (Now, they don't have to paint the ship nearly as often.) Afterward, the entire crew got to celebrate with a steak dinner.

Andy Stanley is another leader who uses Dorothy's Way. He is lead pastor at North Point Community Church in the Atlanta area. He has creative teams that lead various areas of the church, and he serves on some of those teams, listening, encouraging, interpreting what he hears, and then—only then— pointing the way and displaying courage to step into the future. In less than ten years, North Point has grown to 18,000 people in attendance each Sunday. He doesn't claim to be a Wizard. Just an ordinary person, like Dorothy, who won't let those gifted people fall short of what they have inside them.

Maybe some of us are trying hard to be something we're not. Maybe we're imitating styles of leadership that are becoming outdated. Maybe those around us aren't looking for a Wizard after all. And maybe the best thing that could happen to us would be to have someone pull back the curtain and reveal we aren't superheroes, but regular men and women who want to take a journey and reach a destination with a team. I believe we'll find we can do it if we lead Dorothy's Way.

A Look at the Book

I find it intriguing that this new way of leading isn't new at all. Jesus didn't come as some Wizard to intimidate us. He came as a servant, feeding, listening, healing, forming a team of twelve, mentoring them, and washing their feet. And they turned the world upside down (Acts 17:6). Check out the book of Luke, and note the times you see Jesus leading Dorothy's Way in this book.

1. How did He model listening?

_____

_____

_____

2. How did He model encouraging?

_____

_____

_____

3. How did He model serving?

_____

_____

_____

4. How did He model empowerment and identifying gifts in others?

_____

_____

_____

5. How did He model resolve or courage?

_____

_____

_____

Getting Personal

In reality, Frank Baum's story *The Wizard of Oz* was a commentary on the economic and political times at the turn of the 20th century. The scarecrow represented the farmers who were perceived as folks without a brain; the tin man represented industry, who didn't seem to have any heart; the cowardly lion symbolized William Jennings Bryan whom Baum felt lacked the courage to stand up to the wrongs in Washington D.C. The wizard was the federal government—who didn't really have the answers everyone sought. And Dorothy represented the average American who showed her friends they actually had what it took to reach their dreams.[1] Leadership resides in each of us.

Take a moment and evaluate how you model Dorothy's Way with your team.

1. How do you spot the gifts inside your team, like courage, intellect, and heart?

_____

_____

_____

2. How do you listen and seek wisdom from your team and from outsiders?

_____

_____

_____

3. How do you coach and empower your team members?

_____

_____

_____

4. How do you display courage and resolve to reach your goals?

_____

_____

_____

5. How do you serve your team members?

_____

_____

_____

Practicing the Truth

Take a look at your answers to the five questions above. This week, practice one item from each of your responses. Practice spotting gifts, listening, coaching and empowering, modeling courage, and serving your team—without announcing to them you're going to do so. Model Dorothy's Way. At the end of the week, ask if anyone saw any differences in your leadership style. Talk about it.

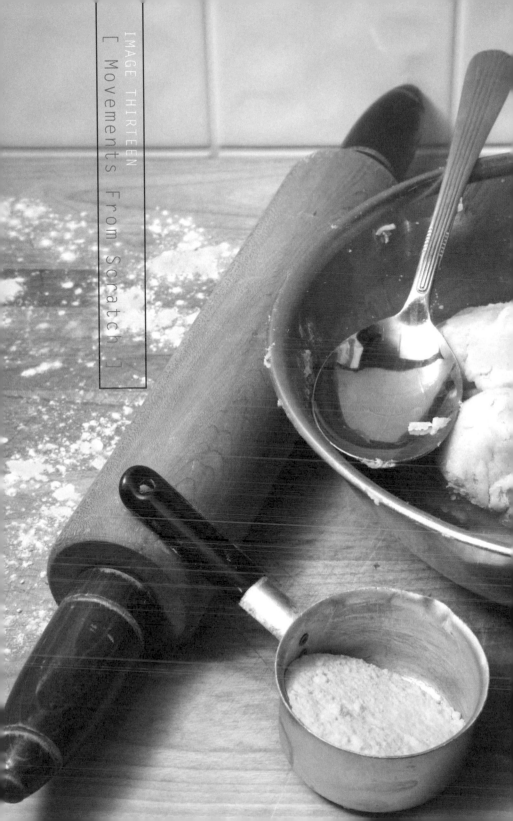

Movements From Scratch

MOVEMENTS VARY, BUT THE ELEMENTS DON'T. GOD'S PATTERN FOR STARTING A CONTAGIOUS MOVEMENT IS: CENTRAL MAN, COMPELLING MISSION, CORE MEMBERS, CREATIVE MODEL, CATALYTIC MEETING, CRITICAL MASS, AND COMMUNITY MATERIALS.

Growing up, I remember my grandmother inviting her grandkids to help her bake a chocolate cake from scratch. You know what that meant. We all washed our hands, and then proceeded to make the biggest mess ever in her kitchen. We got out the flour, fresh milk, fresh eggs, butter, cocoa and sugar and began blending them into Grandma's big mixing bowl. Two hours later, we announced to the rest of the family that our masterpiece was ready to be consumed. With a little help from Grandma, we had created a cake from nothing. There was no boxed cake mix involved in this project. It was all raw ingredients.

Using a cake mix would have been an easy way and a faster route to reach our goal, but it also would have been far less rewarding. We wanted to be able to say our cake was made from all natural ingredients (nothing was artificial), and it took lots of hard work! A boxed cake mix would have felt fake, especially since we made it in our Grandma's house.

In the same way, a movement that changes the culture of an organization or a society cannot be achieved in an artificial way or by taking the easy, fast route. Do you remember our conclusion about the difference between programs and movements? Programs usually start big, then fizzle eventually. They are like a boxed cake mix. They aren't bad; they're just not organic. Just add water and stir. They're fast and easy, but they don't have the same quality. Movements that instigate real change are organic, like baking a cake from scratch. They require more work and they take more time—but their quality is superior, their ingredients are natural, and they last longer.

Basic Ingredients in a Movement

Over the years, I have studied various movements in history; movements that changed the culture of organizations and societies. Each of these movements in history teach us something about how humans change; how lifestyles and laws and patterns of behavior are transformed. From Europe to Asia, from the Middle Ages to the present day, from the abolitionist movement in the 18th century to the Civil Rights movement in the 20th century—these revolutions share some common ingredients. Although God used both men and women, single and married, young and old to pull off these changes, there are some basic ingredients to all of them, just like a good chocolate cake always includes certain ingredients that make it delicious. Note the ingredients below:

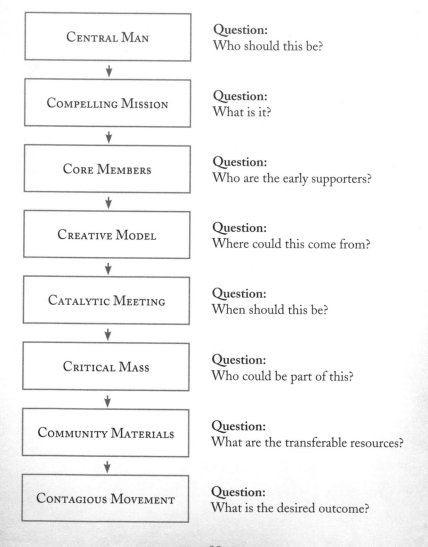

CENTRAL MAN	Question: Who should this be?
COMPELLING MISSION	Question: What is it?
CORE MEMBERS	Question: Who are the early supporters?
CREATIVE MODEL	Question: Where could this come from?
CATALYTIC MEETING	Question: When should this be?
CRITICAL MASS	Question: Who could be part of this?
COMMUNITY MATERIALS	Question: What are the transferable resources?
CONTAGIOUS MOVEMENT	Question: What is the desired outcome?

First, God puts His finger on a **central man or woman**. This individual becomes the catalyst for a needed change. Generally, they begin alone and go against the status quo. God usually doesn't start with a committee or a massive crowd. Most of the time, it's one person.

Next, this person develops a **compelling mission**. He or she summarizes the vision into a brief, simple statement that captures the change they want to make. It is easy to understand, so many can join in along the way. This easy-to-grasp message becomes a mantra for the movement.

Third, this central individual gathers a cadre of people who share his or her convictions. They, too, want to see change, but need a person to get something started. These **core members** build synergy in their group. They're most valuable when they share diverse skills, but a similar vision. They are the supporting cast that keeps the flame burning.

Fourth, this core group identifies a **creative model** from the past. They find some group of people that were able to change an organization or country in history, and say, "See, God did it before, He can do it again." This model becomes a source of encouragement and inspiration.

Next, this central individual and the core people promote the mission effectively enough to pique the curiosity of many. These people are invited to participate in a **catalytic meeting**. This meeting becomes the launching pad, where the mission moves from "idea" to "action."

Sixth, although many hear the mission summarized at the catalytic meeting, not everyone "signs up" to get involved. A percentage of people do, however, and they make up the **critical mass**. The critical mass may be small, but they're a percentage that buys in with high commitment. This percentage returns home with the virus and spread this movement in their particular locale.

Finally, along the way, the percentage of people involved grows. The original group spreads to many places and multiplies the ideas of the young movement in small groups. The original leader recognizes the mission must have a duplicable resource. To insure the mission isn't diluted, **community materials** are created. The ideas become transferable concepts.

Eventually, this group of changed people begins infecting a larger body of the population. The movement spreads beyond the boundaries of the original few and it remains beyond the life of the original leader. Months and years pass, and it becomes a **contagious movement**.

During the 1700s, John Wesley followed this pattern to the letter in England. He was asked to leave the Anglican Church, but soon began a movement called Methodism. As a young man, he wanted to see spiritual renewal in the land, and to see people live holy lives before God. He soon had a cadre of others on board, including his brother, Charles, and some friends from Oxford.

His creative model was the Moravians, who experienced this renewal in Europe. He pointed to them as the example that it could be done! Eventually, John rode his horse around England in a circuit, holding catalytic meetings. A percentage of folks responded to his message, which he organized into small groups called "class meetings." These groups met regularly for accountability and support. Because the numbers grew so large and because Wesley was aging, he knew he had to commit his ideals to print. He began training ordinary laymen to preach and spread this movement—and it worked. In fact, he was so methodical, England began to call him the great "Methodist."[1] His church movement still exists to this day.

Susan B. Anthony had her own vision: women's rights. She devoted herself almost exclusively to this cause from 1854 on, building a core of people including Elizabeth Stanton and Amelia Bloomer. She and Elizabeth traveled thousands of miles making speeches, gathering folks to the cause. Susan averaged 75 to 100 speeches a year for forty-five years. In 1869, she founded the "National Women's Suffrage Association" which promoted women's rights. Eventually, Susan got the opportunity to address the government, though she always felt self-conscious about her inability to speak well. Due to the momentum she'd garnered, she put her ideals in print in a weekly paper called "The Revolution" whose motto was: *The True Republic: men, their rights and nothing more; women, their rights and nothing less.* Thanks to her pioneer work, women won the right to vote in 1920.[2]

Lech Walesa led a movement a little closer to our time. This feisty electrician was the leader of the Solidarity movement in Poland, which eventually broke the Communist rule in 1989. His compelling mission was free trade unions. After being fired from his job in 1980, he climbed over the wall of the Lenin Shipyard to join the occupation strike. This was the catalytic meeting. With his electrifying personality, he quickly became the leader of the movement. In the next several years, the fight for solidarity collected ten million members. The fight went back and forth between the government and the workers. Over the years, Marshall Law went into effect, and Walesa was interned for eleven months in a remote country house. He was released in November 1982. In 1983, Walesa won a Nobel Peace Prize drawing the world's attention to their struggle. In 1988, strike negotiations resumed and the movement won more freedom. By August 1989, just nine years after Lech climbed the shipyard wall, Poland got its first non-Communist Prime Minister in more than forty years. An unintended result of the movement was not only a new government in Poland, but also the fall of other Communist regimes.[3] Momentum can be a movement's best friend.

Not every movement includes every ingredient in the recipe. But it's amazing how often the same ingredients show up when a movement starts from scratch. The more of these seven ingredients you include, the more likely you are to see the movement last. May God give you His recipe for your place and time.

A Look at the Book

Check out the story of King Josiah, in 2 Chronicles 34-35. Josiah was only eight years old when he became King of Judah. While he was still a teenager, he launched a movement that returned the people of Israel back to their God. It was a spiritual renewal that affected the entire country. Notice the ingredients in his revolution:

A. CENTRAL MAN – Josiah

B. COMPELLING MISSION – Spiritual renewal for Judah

C. CORE MEMBERS – The elders

D. CREATIVE MODEL – King Hezekiah and former stories in Israel's past

E. CATALYTIC MEETING – The meeting outside the Temple

F. CRITICAL MASS – A large percentage of the population (which accelerated the change)

G. COMMUNITY MATERIALS – The Book of the Law (the Scriptures)

H. CONTAGIOUS MOVEMENT – The spiritual reform of God's people

1. After reading these chapters, what stands out in your mind? What are the highlights?

_____

_____

_____

2. What do you think gave a young leader like Josiah the passion to lead such a renewal?

_____

_____

_____

3. Can you think of other modern day movements that included some or all of these ingredients?

_____

_____

_____

Getting Personal

Evaluate what changes are needed in your organization. Or, what are the changes needed in your community? Now, evaluate what ingredients are in place or are still needed to launch a movement:

A. Central Man (or woman):

_____

_____

_____

B. Compelling Mission:

_____

_____

_____

C. Core Members:

_____

_____

_____

D. Creative Model:

_____

_____

_____

E. Catalytic Meeting:

_____

_____

_____

F. CRITICAL MASS:

_____

_____

_____

G. COMMUNITY MATERIALS:

_____

_____

_____

PRACTICING THE TRUTH

Based on what you wrote down above, take some time with your team and discuss what steps you need to take to make progress in changing your culture. What ingredients are missing? Which ones are in place? Pray to determine what actions will launch a movement in partnership with God.

[End Notes]

IMAGE ONE: THE JOSHUA PROBLEM

1 Robert P. Gandossy and Nidhi Verma, "Passing the Torch of Leadership," *Executive Forum*, Spring 2006.

2 Anne Deering, Robert Dilts, Julian Russell, "Leadership Cults and Cultures," *Leader to Leader*, Spring 2003, No. 28. <http://www.pfdf.org/leaderbooks/ L2L/spring2003/deering.html>

3 Robert P. Gandossy and Nidhi Verma, "Passing the Torch of Leadership," *Executive Forum*, Spring 2006.

4 IDEA File, *Communicators Journal*, Winter 1990, 12.

IMAGE TWO: CRITICAL MASS

1 Malcolm Gladwell, *The Tipping Point* (New York: Little Brown and Company), 2002, 34.

2 Ibid, 3-5.

IMAGE THREE: THE HOLLYWOOD EFFECT

1 John Fischer, *Real Believers Ask Why*, (Bethany House Publishers: Minneapolis, MN), 1989, p. 57.

2 "Konstantin Stanislavski," <http://en.wikipedia.org/wiki/Konstantin_Stanislavski>

IMAGE FOUR: FAMILY VIRUS

1 "Bird Flu Cluster," *The Associated Press*, May 25, 2005.

2 James Surowiecki, *The Wisdom of Crowds*, (Random House Publishers), 2004, 40-49.

IMAGE FIVE: PORTABLE TRUTHS

1 Malcolm Gladwell, *The Tipping Point* (New York: Little Brown and Company), 2002, 98.

2 "The Navigators, Our History-The Early Days" <http://www.navigators.org/ us/aboutus/items/missionvisionvalues/items/ Our%20History%20-%20The%20Early%20Days>

IMAGE SIX: TRADE-OFFS

1 Chris Roush, "Pillow Fight," *Business North Carolina*, December 2003. <www.businessnc.com/archives/2003/12/pillowtex.html>

[2] Al Ries, "Narrow Your Focus to Broaden Your Business," *Innovation Network: Articles & Reports.* <www.thinksmart.com/2/articles/MP_2-2-5.html>

IMAGE SEVEN: GROWING PAINS

[1] The Coca-Cola Company website:
<http://www2.coca-cola.com/heritage/chronicle_the_candler_era.html>
<http://www2.coca-cola.com/ourcompany/historybottling.html>

IMAGE EIGHT: GIFT FACTOR

[1] "Jacques Nasser," <http://en.wikipedia.org/wiki/Jacques_Nasser> <www.automotivedigest.com/include/2901.html#LookingForLegends>

[2] "Cinderella Man," 2005.<www.imdb.com/title/tt0352248/plotsummary>

[3] Alice Gray, *Stories For The Heart*, (Sisters, Oregon: Multnomah Publishers), 2000, 54-55.

IMAGE NINE: SCIENCE CLASS

[1] Brent Schlender, *Fortune*, editor-at-large, "Pixar's Magic Man," May 17, 2006. <http://money.cnn.com/2006/05/15/magazines/fortune/pixar_futureof_fortune_052906/index.htm>

IMAGE TEN: THE RIPPLE EFFECT

[1] Malcolm Gladwell, *The Tipping Point*, (New York: Little Brown and Company), 2002, 133-146.

[2] Chris Armstrong, "Simeon's Brigade," *Leadership*, Summer, 2003.

IMAGE ELEVEN: CATHEDRAL BUILDING

[1] Jeffrey Baumgartner, "Communication and Innovation," *Report 103*, March 2, 2004. <www.jpb.com/creative/articlecommunication.php>

IMAGE TWELVE: DOROTHY'S WAY

[1] Henry M. Littlefield, "The Wizard of Oz: Parable on Populism," *American Quarterly 16* (1964): 47-58.

IMAGE THIRTEEN: MOVEMENTS FROM SCRATCH

[1] "History of the Methodist Church," *A Brief History of Methodism.* <http://www.methodist.org.uk/index.cfm?fuseaction=welcome.content&cmid=12>

[2] "Susan B. Anthony," <http://en.wikipedia.org/wiki/Susan_Anthony>

[3] "Lech Walesa," <www.time.com/time/time100/leaders/profile/walesa3.html>

Acknowledgements

Special thanks goes to Bethany Deidel and Chris Moore who added valuable thoughts and research to this book. Their work made this project worthwhile. In addition, I appreciate the editing work of Anne Alexander, who made the book understandable. Also, thanks to Bethany Elmore and Sarah Hodgkinson for their work on the images. Your work made this book memorable. Finally, special thanks to Brad Scholle for his finishing work on this book. I appreciate you very much.

Tim